The Right Use of Moral Philosophy

SOURCES IN EARLY MODERN ECONOMICS, ETHICS, AND LAW

Second Series

GENERAL EDITORS

Andrew M. McGinnis Wim Decock
Junius Institute • USA   KU Leuven • Belgium

Continuing in the line of its predecessor, this series publishes original English translations and editions of early modern religious texts in the disciplines of economics, ethics, and law. Representing a variety of confessional traditions and methodological approaches, these texts uncover the foundations of the development of these and related disciplines.

EDITORIAL BOARD

Jordan J. Ballor
Acton Institute • USA

Christiane Birr
Max Planck Institute for European Legal History • Germany

Stephen Bogle
University of Glasgow • Scotland

Alejandro Chafuen
Acton Institute • USA

Ricardo F. Crespo
Universidad Austral and CONICET • Argentina

Virpi Mäkinen
University of Helsinki • Finland

Richard A. Muller
Calvin Theological Seminary • USA

Herman Selderhuis
Theological University Apeldoorn • The Netherlands

John Witte Jr.
Emory Law School • USA

Zhibin Xie
Tongji University • China

The Right Use of Moral Philosophy
Pierre de la Place

Translated by Albert Gootjes
Introduction by Martin I. Klauber

GRAND RAPIDS · MICHIGAN

The Right Use of Moral Philosophy

Translation © 2021 by Albert Gootjes

Introduction © 2021 by Martin I. Klauber

All rights reserved. No part of this publication may be reproduced, stored in a retrieval system, or transmitted in any form or by any means, including electronic, mechanical, photocopying, recording, or otherwise without the prior permission of the publisher.

ISBN 978-1-949011-06-7 (hardcover)
ISBN 978-1-949011-07-4 (paperback)
ISBN 978-1-949011-08-1 (ebook)

CLP Academic
  *An imprint of the Acton Institute
  for the Study of Religion & Liberty*
98 E. Fulton
Grand Rapids, Michigan 49503
616.454.3080
www.acton.org

Interior composition by Judy Schafer
Cover design by Scaturro Design

Contents

Preface   *xi*

Introduction   *xv*

The Right Use of Moral Philosophy

Epistle   3

Book One

1. The excellence of the science of morals over all human sciences   11

2. The bad that results from the confusion of the science of morals with Christian doctrine; and how the Epicureans, sophists, and scholastics, and even the first and most ancient church fathers, have misused it   13

3. All human actions and deliberations have an end; the diversity of ends, and how the remotest end is the most excellent and that in which the sovereign good resides   16

4. The order for arriving at knowledge of the sovereign good, and what those who want to be students of the science of morals ought to be like   17

5. The excellence of the sovereign good is more apparent in the science of politics, and also more necessary for it than for all other sciences   19

6. The sovereign good is called felicity, and what true felicity is   19

7. The felicity of the life of pleasure, and Epicurus's view of it   20

8. The felicity of political life   21

9. Aristotle's view of felicity   22

10. Plato's view of felicity   23

11. The most common view among philosophers concerning human felicity, and true felicity according to Christian doctrine   24

12. The tranquility and contentment of the mind are not true felicity   27

13. Felicity is located in the soul, and not in bodily and external goods, and how the sovereign good of the Christian surpasses them all   28

14. The cause of felicity according to Aristotle, and according to the truth of Christian doctrine   29

Book Two

1. Democritus's view of good and bad images in the air   35

2. The science of morality must consider human nature, and Plato's view of it   36

3. The partition and division of the soul according to Plato and Aristotle   36

4. The partition and division of virtues according to Plato and Aristotle, and that neither Plato nor Aristotle had knowledge of the principal intellectual virtues   38

5. The principal, Christian intellectual virtues   40

6. The moral virtues, and, in the first place, how they are acquired, namely, whether it is by nature or by works   41

7. The science of morality resides more in the exercise and performance of good works, and not in knowledge, and the treatment of moral virtues by philosophy, provided that it is properly understood, does not conflict with Christian doctrine   43

8. By what works virtue is acquired, and how virtue,
   once acquired, produces works that fully resemble those
   from which it was first produced   44

9. The way to know when the habit of virtue will be formed
   in someone   45

10. Habit is primarily concerned with pleasure and displeasure,
    and how humanity's true institution concerns
    these two points   46

11. We must not locate the end of pleasure and displeasure
    in ourselves   47

12. The task of virtue, and the false view of the Stoics
    in this regard   47

13. The proper nature of virtue concerns pleasure and displeasure,
    and the main difficulty is discerning and choosing well
    between the two   48

14. Whether one becomes good by doing good works,
    or whether one must first be good to do what is good   49

15. People usually derive greater pleasure from knowing good
    things than from doing them   51

16. The will, and a person's inner parts that precede it   52

17. Deliberation   52

18. Choice, and how it is not the same thing as will, pleasure,
    or opinion   53

19. The will, what ought to be called voluntary or forced,
    and the difference between something done by ignorance
    and something done ignorantly   54

20. Comparison between human justification according to
    Christian doctrine and the justification taught
    by philosophy   55

21. How human beings have always been inclined to attribute justice to their works, and how the error of the scholastics' view arose from philosophy   57

Book Three

1. What virtue is, whether it is affection, power, or habit   64

2. Virtue is habit, and what this habit is   65

3. The arithmetic method and the geometric method   66

4. The geometric method applies to all arts and sciences, and how moral virtue relates to it and intellectual virtue does not   67

5. Virtue is an intermediate point between excess and deficiency, and why it is more difficult to do good than evil   68

6. The definition of virtue according to Aristotle, and how not every action or affection in itself admits an intermediate point   69

7. The definition of virtue condensed, and then appropriated in accordance with Christian doctrine   70

8. The difference between the treatment of things that reside in simple knowledge, and those that reside in action   71

9. Each virtue taken on its own consists in an intermediate point, and on their names and extremes   71

10. The intermediate point that consists in affections and passions, which is nevertheless no virtue   73

11. The contrariety between the two extremes of the intermediate point and the mean, and the contrariety between the mean and its extremes, and also the resemblance between these extremes and the mean   74

12. The intermediate point that we maintain always inclines
    more to one extreme than to the other, and the most
    certain rule for better maintaining the mean in all things   76

13. Arming oneself against the vices to which we are most
    inclined, and especially against delights and pleasures   77

14. The view of the Peripatetics and Stoics on the affections
    and their intermediate points, and how their reasons differ
    more in word than substance   78

15. Whether according to philosophy it is in us to do good
    or evil, and whether it is in us to refrain from evil   81

16. Comparison between Christian doctrine and philosophy
    on the will to do good and the will to do evil, and how
    philosophy has failed to recognize the source and cause
    of human sin   86

17. The great impediment to the freedom of the human will
    in matters pertaining to the present life, and how one
    ought to profit from the fall of great men   88

18. Internal and spiritual movements are not from us   89

19. Whether it is possible for people to act according
    to God's law, and how statesmen ought to take no offense
    at this teaching   90

20. The order of virtues maintained by Cicero differs
    from Aristotle's   91

Index   93

Preface

As Martin Klauber writes in his introduction to this volume, the Huguenot reformer Pierre de la Place is "more well-known for his martyrdom than his life." Albert Gootjes's translation of La Place's *Du droict usage de la philosophie morale avec la doctrine chrestienne*, together with Klauber's carefully researched introduction, sheds new light on the life and contributions of this often overlooked French reformer. Since La Place was significant in his own time and context but generally neglected in modern scholarship, and since *Du droict usage de la philosophie morale* addresses the relationship between ethics and Christian theology, the treatise is well suited for the Sources in Early Modern Economics, Ethics, and Law series.

The title of this English edition, *The Right Use of Moral Philosophy*, is an abbreviated rendering of the complete French title, which could be translated as "The right use of moral philosophy with Christian doctrine" or, a bit more verbose, "On the proper way to use moral philosophy with Christian doctrine." Although we have opted for a crisper English title, it is important to remember that La Place's purpose was not merely to sketch the contours of moral philosophy, but to distinguish between the disciplines of moral philosophy and theology without separating them. By properly distinguishing between these two disciplines (or sciences), La Place hoped to promote and advance both of them, though in this work he is chiefly concerned with moral philosophy and the pursuit of virtue. In *The Right Use of Moral Philosophy*, therefore, we have an early Reformed Protestant account of ethics as a discipline with its own principles and methods that differ from, and should not be confused with, those of dogmatics. The source text for this translation is the first French edition, published by Frédéric Morel in 1562. At points the translator compared this text with the 1587 Latin edition, published by Eustache Vignon. The French text is taken as authoritative since it is the only edition to appear in La Place's lifetime. The Latin translation omits La Place's epistle to Michel de l'Hôpital, and it adds chapter breaks that differ from the French edition. In fact, no chapter or section breaks appear in the body text of the French edition, but the table of contents does indicate the location of such breaks with section headings and their respective beginning folio numbers. In this English translation these section breaks and headings have been inserted into the body text at their proper locations, and section numbers have been added accordingly. The section headings are therefore original in the sense that they appear in the original table of contents. The French edition also contains marginal glosses throughout, which have not been included here.

All of the footnotes are editorial additions intended to help the modern reader identify La Place's references and sources. Since La Place did not provide citations, the notes can only suggest the most likely sources he had in mind. He seems to have been relying on memory for many of his classical references, though there is no way to know for certain what texts he might have had at hand. When La Place refers to a classical figure or event, or to a figure in Christian history, usually a brief description is added in a note. Unless otherwise indicated, the dates and biographical information about classical figures and events are taken from *The Oxford Classical Dictionary*, edited by Simon Hornblower, Antony Spawforth, and Esther Eidinow, 4th ed. (Oxford: Oxford University Press, 2012). In rendering La Place's quotations of classical texts, the translator has used modern English editions when the French text does not depart too far from the original Greek or Latin. In each case the English edition is indicated in a footnote.

I would like to thank the translator, Albert Gootjes, and the introducer, Martin Klauber, for their excellent work in making La Place accessible to an English readership. It was a pleasure to work with such fine historians of the early modern period. I also owe a debt of gratitude to several individuals who helped put this edition into final form. Matthew W. Wright assisted in the editing of the English text and spent many hours (including a few road trips to Fresno State's library) researching editorial notes. David Noe read the whole manuscript with a classicist's eye, and he went above and beyond the call of duty by offering many revisions that improved the text's readability and clarity. At a late stage in the editorial process, Alden McCray led a reading group through the manuscript and passed along the group's comments, which spurred a few last-minute tweaks to the text. Lastly, I would like to thank my series co-general editor, Wim Decock, for his collegiality and partnership in this endeavor, and for his patience when I have filled his inbox with e-mails.

— Andrew M. McGinnis

"Assassination of La Place," by Joseph Martin Kronheim (1810–1896). From *Book of Martyrs*, by John Foxe, illustrated by Kronheim (London and New York: Frederick Warne and Co., 1887).

INTRODUCTION

Martin I. Klauber

Pierre de la Place (ca. 1520–1572) was an influential early Huguenot reformer who was assassinated a few days following the St. Bartholomew's Day Massacre in 1572. Originally from Angoulême, his family was quite prominent. His father, also named Pierre de la Place, served in the function of mayor and as a financial manager for Louise de Savoie, regent of France and mother of Francis I. He helped arrange the engagement between Francis I and Claude of France and helped to negotiate the king's release after the Battle of Pavia in 1527. Trained as a lawyer at Poitiers, where he met a young John Calvin, and then at Paris, the younger La Place made a name for himself by paraphrasing some of the *Institutiones* of Justinian in 1542.[1] This particular work initially circulated among friends and was eventually published in 1546. La Place practiced law at the *parlement* of Paris beginning when he was only twenty-two, and became so distinguished in his service that King Francis I appointed him as his attorney at the *Cour des aides* in Paris. This was a court that heard cases concerning public finance and customs duties. It was housed at the *Palais Vieux* in Paris. Eventually, he rose in the ranks to become the president of the *Cour des aides*. While practicing law, he began to study the works of Calvin and to look at some of the differences between Roman Catholicism and the

---

[1] Pierre de la Place, *Paraphrasis in titulos institutionum imperialium de actionibus, exceptionibus et interdictis Scholiis seorsum margini appositis* (Paris: Galiot du Pré, 1546).

Reformed faith without initially deciding which side had more merit. However, he may have delayed his decision to embrace the Reformed cause, possibly because of the potential cost to his career and even his life.[2]

La Place did not openly declare his profession of the Reformed faith until 1560, and he then began to study the Christian faith in earnest, even though the political situation was quite unstable. The Queen Mother, Catherine de Medici, was not powerful enough to control the noble factions who opposed each other on religious grounds. She had four sons, three of whom would eventually accede to the French throne, and she faced the difficult task of navigating the crown through political turmoil and factionalism. Her greatest threat came from her sons' uncles, Francis, the duke of Guise, and Charles, the cardinal of Lorraine, who held extensive influence over the young king, Francis II. On the other side of the spectrum were the Protestant leaders Antoine de Navarre, king of Bourbon, and Louis de Bourbon, prince of Condé. The Guise faction advocated the suppression of the so-called Protestant heresy in France and was leading royal policy in that direction. The Huguenots recognized the threat, and the prince of Condé was ready to take action against the Guises.[3]

Such action took the form of an attempt to liberate the king, Francis II, from the Guises by kidnapping him, as the Catholic faction would put it, or freeing him, as the Protestants contended, from their control. The attempt took place at the king's castle at Amboise on the Loire River when Jean de Barrie, seigneur de la Renaudie, along with several hundred armed members of the nobility attempted to storm the castle on March 17, 1560. They were defeated by the forces led by the duke of Guise, who had been tipped off about the operation in advance. La Renaudie was captured, drawn and quartered, and between 1,200 and

---

[2] Eugène Haag and Émile Haag, *La France Protestante: ou vies des protestants français qui se sont fait un nom dans l'Histoire depuis les premiers temps de la réformation jusqu'à la reconnaissance du principe de la liberté des cultes par l'assemblée nationale*, vol. 6 (Paris: Joël Cherbuliez, 1857), 312.

[3] Mack P. Holt, *The French Wars of Religion, 1562–1629*, 2nd ed. (Cambridge: Cambridge University Press, 2005), 45–48.

1,500 of his followers were executed with their bodies hanged from hooks on the castle walls or from trees for the townspeople to view. This so-called Amboise Conspiracy had the support of the prince of Condé, but the Genevans, led by Calvin, attempted to discourage the plot. The prince of Condé was eventually arrested in October 1560 for his role in the affair and was set to be put to death when Francis II died in December from an ear abscess. The new king was his younger brother Charles IX, and Catherine de Medici took advantage of the situation by removing the Guises from power and releasing Condé from prison. The entire affair was a disaster for the Protestant cause as it confirmed for many in France that they were, indeed, seditious.[4]

In 1561, the Queen Mother adopted a position of moderation, much to the dismay of the Guise faction. She appointed Antoine, the king of Navarre, who had a claim to the regency by virtue of his position as first prince of the blood, as lieutenant-general of the realm, and second-in-command of the military after the constable Anne de Montmorency. She also appointed Gaspard de Coligny, a Huguenot who had not supported the Amboise Conspiracy, to the royal council. In response, on Easter Sunday 1561, Francis of Guise, Anne de Montmorency, and Jacques d'Ablon, marshal of St. André, gathered together to form what became known as the "Triumvirate" dedicated to defend the Roman Catholic faith with the assistance of Philip II of Spain.[5]

Catherine countered on April 19 by issuing an edict at Fontainebleau granting limited toleration for the Huguenots by allowing them to worship freely within their own homes. The Protestants desired permission to build their own church buildings and to worship publicly. The royal council and the *parlement* of Paris countered by outlawing even private, home-based worship, but providing a general amnesty for previous violations of religious restrictions. So, the Queen Mother's edict never took effect.[6]

---

[4] Holt, *The French Wars of Religion*, 43–45.

[5] R. J. Knecht, *The French Wars of Religion, 1559–1698*, 3rd ed. (London: Routledge, 2010), 30.

[6] Knecht, *The French Wars of Religion*, 30.

Introduction

In a countermove, Catherine, with the assistance of the chancellor Michel de l'Hôpital, called the Colloquy of Poissy in September 1561 to see if there were grounds for theological compromise. Theodore Beza and Peter Martyr Vermigli led the Protestant delegation of twelve theologians while the Roman Catholic delegation included six cardinals and forty bishops and archbishops. Charles IX and the royal family attended the proceedings with the goal of achieving some kind of accord that could lead to peace, but the two sides were too far apart theologically to come to a resolution. Beza delivered the first full-length oration and attempted to show the areas where the two sides could agree, but on the issue of Christ's physical presence in the elements of communion, he famously said that the body of Christ "is as far away from the bread and wine as the highest heavens are from the earth." At this, the prelates cried out *"blasphemavit!"* meaning "he has blasphemed." Soon after this speech the papal legate Ippolito d'Este, the archbishop of Ferrara, and Diego Laynez, the general superior of the Jesuit order, arrived in an attempt to frustrate the goals of the Colloquy. When one attempt to reconcile the two sides based on the Confession of Augsburg had failed, it was inevitable that the two sides would not come to an agreement.[7]

In January 1562, the Queen Mother issued the Edict of St. Germain, which provided Protestants the right to hold peaceful worship services outside city walls in the countryside. It forbade them to raise arms or to worship at night for fear of armed insurrection, but this was a major step in favor of the Huguenots. The *parlement* of Paris delayed registering the edict and protested against it, forcing the young king to issue a formal royal command to do so, which *parlement* reluctantly did in March 1562.[8]

The drumbeat of war accelerated with the Massacre of Vassy on March 1, 1562, when Francis, the duke of Guise, along with his entourage, was on his way to Sunday Mass near his estate in northeastern France. They came upon some Huguenots worshiping in a barn and tried to force their way in. They were pushed back, but rocks were

---

[7] Knecht, *The French Wars of Religion*, 30–32.
[8] Holt, *The French Wars of Religion*, 48–49.

thrown and the duke was hit. He then ordered the barn to be set on fire. Sixty-three worshipers were killed and more than a hundred wounded. Reaction among the Protestants ranged from anger to shock, and many among the Huguenot nobility began to organize militarily for fear that they would be the next targets. They were led by Admiral Gaspard de Coligny and Louis, prince of Condé, who ostensibly vowed to protect the king from malicious councilors such as the duke of Guise and his supporters. Condé contended that the young king and his mother were being held hostage by the Guises and proceeded to take the city of Orléans on April 2, 1562.[9]

In the midst of all of this religious and political turmoil, La Place had to count very carefully the cost of his beliefs. It would have been professionally advantageous for him to remain in the Roman Catholic faith. However, he was a convinced Protestant, and he quickly recognized that he would do better to leave Paris for Picardy where his family owned some property. Discharged from his position at the *Cour des aides*, he took advantage of his situation and began to study the Christian faith in depth as well as the classical authors of antiquity. He also cared for the land and tutored his children. He expressed his desire to provide the best possible education for them in the love of God and desired to compose some brief treatises in part to assist them in this endeavor. According to Eugène and Émile Haag, the *Droict usage de la philosophie morale avec la doctrine chrestienne*[10] was designed for such a purpose.[11] He also published an interesting work dedicated to Charles IX, his *Traitté de la vocation*, which was translated into

---

[9] Holt, *The French Wars of Religion*, 49–50.

[10] Pierre de la Place, *Du droict usage de la philosophie morale avec la doctrine chrestienne* (Paris: Morel, 1562). Subsequent references to *Du droict usage* include corresponding references to the present English edition, *The Right Use of Moral Philosophy*.

[11] Haag and Haag, *La France Protestante*, 312.

English in 1578 and into Latin in 1587.[12] In the dedication, he advised Charles IX that the best quality of a good leader is his ability to choose his advisors and officials wisely. A wise monarch, he argued, must be able to discern which public servants wish to advance their own personal or dynastic interests to the detriment of the realm. La Place went on to counter Cicero's contention that one's vocation is dependent on one's spirit, natural inclination, and the chance of fortune. La Place, instead, argued that it is really divine providence rather than the vagaries of fortune that leads one to the proper vocation. What is interesting about his argument is that La Place asserted that God has a vocational calling for all of his people, whatever their profession might be. It would not just be a calling for a career in the church or the political realm, but in any endeavor. La Place did endorse succession as the most effective way of choosing a monarch, but seemed to take a swipe at the Roman Catholic mode of choosing clergy, clearly harkening back to earlier times when the laity played a role in their calling for service. For example, the Levitical priests were brought before the Israelites for consecration in Numbers 8:10 before they were presented before God as a wave offering.[13]

La Place also included an interesting chapter on the administration of the realm in cases of a royal minority. Although he admitted that the Salic law prohibited women from becoming monarchs in their own right, it did not exclude them from administration of the kingdom. He specifically mentioned the legitimacy of Catherine de Medici's role in governance as the Queen Mother. In fact, he praised her as having

---

[12] Pierre de la Place, *Traitté de la vocation et maniere de vivre a laquelle chacun est appellé* (Paris: Morel, 1561); *Politique discourses: treating of the differences and inequalities of vocation, as well publique as private: with the scopes or endes whereunto they are directed*, trans. Ægremont Ratcliffe (London: Edward Aggas, 1578); *De vocatione, seu de ea vivendi ratione ad quam quisque vocatus est, libri tres*, in *Petri Plateani viri clarissimi, in curia parisiensi regiorum subsidiorum, seu vectigalium praesidis primatii, Opuscula* [...] ([Geneva]: Eustathius Vignon, 1587), 109–247.

[13] La Place, *Traitté de la vocation*, 1–12.

come to her position as a result of divine providence and described her as most wise, good, and virtuous.[14]

Although his praise for the Queen Mother likely did not play much of a role in his return to Paris or to an increased measure of religious tolerance for the Protestants, it could not have hurt the cause. La Place was able to return to Paris in 1563 after the Edict of Amboise, also known as the Edict of Pacification, signed by Catherine de Medici on behalf of Charles IX. According to Hugues Daussy, La Place anonymously composed *l'Epistre au roy, sur la faict de la religion* (1564), where he argued that the edict did not go far enough in protecting the rights of the Huguenots.[15]

La Place successfully countered the accusations against him to such an extent that Charles IX returned him to his former position. The prince of Condé followed suit and put him in charge of his household affairs, and La Place served in a role like a modern-day chief of staff.[16] While in the entourage of Condé, La Place understood the necessity of composing an in-depth work on the origins of the religious wars in France, which he expanded into a history of the conflict during the reigns of Henry II, Francis II, and Charles IX. According to Émile and Eugène Haag, this work, La Place's *Commentaires*, was remarkably balanced rather than serving as merely a propaganda piece for the Protestants.[17] It did favor the Huguenots, however, and presented the history from their perspective.[18] According to Myriam Yardeni,

---

[14] La Place, *Traitté de la vocation*, 36–37.

[15] Hugues Daussy, *Le Parti Huguenot: Chronique d'une désillusion (1557–1572)* (Geneva: Droz, 2015), 538.

[16] Haag and Haag, *La France Protestante*, 313.

[17] Haag and Haag, *La France Protestante*, 313; cf. Christoph Strohm, *Ethik im frühen Calvinismus* (Berlin: De Gruyter, 1996), 555; Pierre de la Place, *Commentaires de l'estat de la religion et république sous les rois Henry & François seconds, & Charles neuvième* (n.p.: n.p., 1565).

[18] Myriam Yardeni, "La pensée politique de la première historiographie huguenote: Pierre de la Place et Louis Régnier de La Planche," in *Cité des hommes, cité de Dieu. Travaux sur la littérature de la Renaissance en l'honneur de Daniel Ménager*, ed. Jean Céard et al. (Geneva: Droz, 2003), 104–5.

xxi

Introduction

La Place was very subtle in his use of words. For example, in his discussion of Beza's speech at the Colloquy of Poissy, La Place described him as "modest" in his presentation, which was not likely the case. He also quoted Beza's speech in detail while he included mere summaries or partial citations of the presentations of the Roman Catholic representatives, Cardinal François de Tournon and the cardinal of Lorraine.[19] Furthermore, she points out that he did not attack the papacy directly, but was more constructive, writing from a Gallican perspective and using historical narrative to weave a convincing and sympathetic story. He emphasized that religious belief belongs properly to one's own conscience and really has little to do with the Huguenots' loyalty to the crown. However, religion and politics were inexorably intertwined, and personal belief was a fundamental right, a notion that would take many years to be fulfilled. The notion of the Third Estate was being mistreated and denied, an idea that was in part shared by Michel de l'Hôpital, the royal chancellor, who addressed the States-General in Orléans in 1560.[20]

The *Commentaires* was originally published anonymously, but Jean-François Gilmont has shown that the true author was La Place. The publisher was not listed in the book, but Gilmont has made the plausible argument that Eloi Gibier, the official printer of the prince of Condé, was the sponsor.[21] Daussy argues that this work was the first of a number of historical defenses of the Reformed cause that pointed to the repression that took place starting in 1557. It also was written in a narrative form to ensure a wider audience.[22] Patrick Cabanel points out that the chronological starting point of the book was designed specifically to continue the narrative of Johann Sleidan who had died in 1556 and who had composed the important *Commentaries on the State*

---

[19] Myriam Yardeni, *Minorités et mentalités religieuses en Europe moderne: L'Exemple des Huguenots*, ed. Michael Green (Paris: Honoré Champion, 2018), 57.

[20] Yardeni, *Minorités et mentalités*, 60–62.

[21] Jean-François Gilmont, "Les premières éditions des ouvrages de La Place et de La Popelinère," *Revue française d'histoire du livre* 55 (1986): 120–26.

[22] Daussy, *Le Parti Huguenot*, 45.

INTRODUCTION

of Religion and the Republic under the Emperor Charles V (1556).[23] La Place's work went through a number of editions which were published in Rouen, La Rochelle, and Paris.[24]

La Place composed this treatise from a Huguenot perspective, lamenting various persecutions starting with the arrest of more than a hundred Protestants out of a total of about four hundred who were worshiping in a private home on September 4, 1557, on the rue Saint-Jacques in the Latin Quarter in Paris. Included in the number under arrest were many women of the nobility who were sent to Châtelet prison. He also narrated a detailed and sympathetic account of Anne du Bourg, the Calvinist member of the Paris *parlement* who had urged religious toleration, but was instead arrested for heresy, tried, and executed on December 23, 1559. La Place included a detailed account of Du Bourg's defense, which was a very clever method because he was able to use Du Bourg's words rather than his own. Du Bourg argued that he only believed in the divine inspiration of the Bible and that nothing should be added or subtracted from it, saying that any Roman Catholic doctrines that he opposed were contrary to Scripture. Du Bourg continued that the Lord worked for six days and rested on the seventh and made the Sabbath holy. The pope, however, added certain fast days to the requirement and limited days in which the faithful could eat meat. He also criticized the practice of clerical celibacy, arguing that it went beyond Paul's prescription in 1 Corinthians 7 that only those who have a special gift of continence should refrain from marriage. These are only a few examples from a lengthy work in which La Place placed a Protestant interpretation on this history of the religious conflict.[25] This work went through seven editions and

---

[23] Patrick Cabanel, *Histoire des protestants en France XVIe-XXIe siècle* (Paris: Fayard, 2012), 241; Johannes Sleidanus, *De statu religionis et reipublicae, Carolo Quinto, Caesare, commentarii*, 2 vols. ([Strasbourg]: Rihelius, 1555). On Sleidan, see Alexandra Kess, *Johann Sleidan and the Protestant Vision of History* (Farnham, UK: Ashgate, 2008).

[24] Cabanel, *Histoire des protestants*, 241.

[25] La Place, *Commentaires*, 5-6, 26-29.

xxiii

was translated into Latin in 1572–75 and English in 1573.[26] It was also later included in the multivolume anthology of the history of France, *Choix de chroniques et mémoires sur l'histoire de France*, in 1836.[27]

Unfortunately, the beginning of the third of the so-called Wars of Religion forced La Place to leave Paris again in 1568, his house ransacked, his library disbursed, and his finances frozen. This time he ventured to a castle in Valois belonging to his nephews where he served as a tutor to the children. While at the castle, a warrant was issued for his arrest due to his Protestant beliefs and slanderous accusations that had surfaced about him, and he had to flee and take refuge in the forest. Finally, he found refuge in the home of a sympathetic neighboring lord who allowed him to hide in his castle without any communication with the outside world and without any books to read except the Bible. There, he composed his *Traicté de l'excellence de l'homme chrestien et manière de le cognoistre*, but it was not published until 1575, after his death. It was translated into English in 1576.[28] He dedicated it to the queen of Navarre, Jeanne d'Albret, a noted Huguenot. In this work, he advocated in the most poignant terms yet of all his works for traditional Reformed doctrines such as election, saying,

> Yet notwithstanding, it pleased God, of a certain more than fatherly love, and special favor which he bore him [the Christian], not only even from his birth, and from the first hour he

---

[26] Pierre de la Place, *Commentariorum de statu religionis & reipublicæ in regno Galliæ I. partis libri III. Regibus Henrico secundo ... Francisco secundo, & Carolo nono. Recogniti & plerisque in locis emendati* (n.p.: n.p., 1572–75); *The fyrst parte of commentaries, concerning the state of religion, and the common wealthe of Fraunce, under the reignes of Henry the second, Frauncis the second, and Charles the ninth*, trans. Thomas Tymme (London: Henrie Bynneman, 1573).

[27] J. A. C. Buchon, *Choix de chroniques et mémoires sur l'histoire de France, avec notices biographiques* (Paris: A. Desrez, 1836).

[28] Pierre de la Place, *Traicté de l'excellence de l'homme chrestien et manière de le cognoistre* ([Geneva]: [Jacob Stoer,] 1575); *A treatise of the excellencie of a christian man, and how he may be knowen*, trans. Laurence Tomson (London: Christopher Barker, 1576).

brought him out into this world, but even from his mother's womb, and even before he was conceived, and even before the world was made (as he predestined him to himself from everlasting) to elect and choose him from among an infinite number of men, to mark him and set him apart, to exempt him from the common state and condition of all other men, that is to say, from everlasting condemnation and destruction which was prepared for him, as well as for every other man, to reserve him for himself, to adopt and regenerate him in the hope of life to an incorruptible inheritance kept in store in heaven, to be revealed to his elect on that day when all things shall be restored, and to show in him the riches of his glory, as in a vessel of mercy prepared to salvation.[29]

He defined the excellency of the Christian as not consisting of anything in oneself—and here he cautioned against the view of the "philosophers"—but solely in the grace of God whereby a person is made one with Christ and is regenerated.[30]

When the persecution against the Protestants subsided with the Peace of St. Germain on August 5, 1570, ironically negotiated by the Huguenot Queen of Navarre, Jeanne d'Albret, he was able to return to his home and his post at the *Cour des aides*. However, his tenure there was precarious to say the least and ended in 1572 with the St. Bartholomew's Day Massacre.

Typically a scholar's career is not defined by his death, but La Place's demise was chronicled in Simon de Goulart's *Memoires de l'estat de France sous Charles neufiesme*, and a print of his murder, completed by the nineteenth-century lithographer Joseph Martin Kronheim, was included in the 1887 edition of Foxe's *Book of Martyrs*. As a result, he became more well-known for his martyrdom than for his life. Goulart's three-volume work helped to memorialize the experiences of the

---

[29] La Place, *Traicté de l'excellence*, 19–20 (my translation).
[30] La Place, *Traicté de l'excellence*, 24–25.

Introduction

Huguenot martyrs from 1570 to 1574 and also served as a source for Protestant propaganda, as most martyrologies do.[31]

Living in relative seclusion on the outskirts of Le Marais, La Place first learned of the massacre when a French captain named Michel came to his home to inform him and to warn him of the imminent threat against him and other Huguenots. The captain offered him shelter, but asked how much gold he had in his house, ostensibly asking for payment. La Place replied that the king would not tolerate such actions. In response the captain offered to take him to the king. Realizing the ruse, La Place declined the offer and sneaked out the back door. However, he did pay the official one thousand crowns to hide his wife and children with a Catholic family. Pierre, unfortunately, was unable to find anyone among his neighbors who would hide him from the authorities, and he finally returned home where his wife had already returned. He was worshiping at home on Sunday with his wife, servants, and relatives—ironically, he was commenting on the book of Job and reading Calvin's sermons on it—when the provost, Senescay, arrived with archers to protect him under the orders of the king and to escort him to the Louvre, presumably for safe harbor. However, on the way, the group was attacked, and the soldiers offered no resistance as La Place was stabbed to death. They took his body to the stable at the Hotel-de-Ville where it was thrown into the Seine. His house was then pillaged. It was suspected that a rival, Stephen de Neuilly, helped arrange the murder, in part because he succeeded La Place in his official positions.[32]

La Place intended his *Right Use of Moral Philosophy* to serve as a brief introduction to the topic for his children, but it also seems to have served a wider purpose, namely, to show the superiority of a distinctively Christian statement (and in some ways, a distinctively Protestant statement) of the topic and a presentation of the use of moral philosophy in the public arena. The first edition, upon which

---

[31] See Robert M. Kingdon, *Myths about the St. Bartholomew's Day Massacres, 1572–1576* (Cambridge, MA: Harvard University Press, 1988).

[32] Henry White, *The Massacre of St. Bartholomew: Preceded by a History of the Religious Wars in the Reign of Charles IX* (New York: Harper, 1868), 423–25.

INTRODUCTION

this translation is based, came out in 1562, published in Paris, and included a dedication to Michel de l'Hôpital, who served as chancellor of France from 1560 to 1568. A second edition was published in Leiden in 1658. La Place had a good relationship with L'Hôpital, who had been the president of the *chambre des comptes* from 1555 to 1560. L'Hôpital was a sympathetic figure because he caused the Edict of Romorantin to be registered by the *parlement* of Paris. This edict provided protection for suspected heretics from secret proceedings of the Inquisition. Part of his motivation was to promote a general reform of the French church that would result in unity between the Reformed and the Roman Catholics. Persecution of Protestants would have been counterproductive to such a goal. Furthermore, L'Hôpital set up the council of notables to try to get the States-General to meet, which they finally did following the death of Francis II. This meeting and the endorsement by the new king, Charles IX, and his mother, Catherine de Medici, paved the way for the Colloquy of Poissy and the Edict of St. Germain in 1562, which provided for a much greater degree of tolerance for the fledgling Reformed movement in France. Unfortunately for L'Hôpital, he encountered the opposition of the papal legate, Ippolito d'Este, for a number of reasons including his questioning of the authority of the Council of Trent and his Gallican views on royal power. He also clashed with the Guise faction, most notably the cardinal of Lorraine, over the impact that the imposition of the decree of Trent would have on hard-fought peace with the Protestants in France. Following the Massacre at Vassy, he retired from court life for a brief period until the pacification of Amboise in 1563. Some historians, such as Albert Buisson, have speculated that he was a secret Protestant,[33] but according to Seong-Hak Kim, such assertions are likely based on an uncritical reading of the views of some contemporary Protestants who believed that L'Hôpital was really one of their own. Kim continues to argue that L'Hôpital advocated religious toleration for what he believed was the good of the realm. Both Beza and Calvin, who preferred that if L'Hôpital really were a secret

---

[33] Albert Buisson, *Michel de l'Hospital, 1503–1573* (Paris: Hachette, 1950), 12.

xxvii

Protestant he should come out in the open, recognized his usefulness in support of the Reformed cause.[34]

So, the dedication of this treatise to L'Hôpital was designed to encourage him to follow Scripture as the basis for civil law as a subset of divine law. Natural law, serving as the source of civil law, is also subservient to the overarching authority of divine law. The problem with natural law is that it has often been corrupted by sinful humanity. To reform it, one needs to go back to Scripture as the source of God's ultimate justice. La Place begins the introduction with a bit of an apology for entering into the field of theology when his real training and profession is in the law. However, he points out that divine law has a lot to say on the issue of justice. Theology, he argues, is essential to true justice and to understanding the law truly. Philosophy, he argues, has always been an important component to the acquisition of knowledge, but, citing Tertullian, he says that when mixed with theology it can often be the source of many errors. So, philosophy must be subservient to theology and the Scriptures.[35]

He begins his discussion of moral philosophy relying, ironically, not on the Bible, but on the views of the ancient Greek philosophers. He goes on to condemn the view that one should totally discard the views of the ancient philosophers. Instead, one needs to use them wisely and in accordance with biblical truth. Yet he cautions against excessive reliance upon them and points to the mistakes of some important patristic figures such as Justin Martyr, who refused to give up his philosopher's garb and elevated Plato as a vital source of truth who agreed with a gospel that he never heard. He also is critical of some of the early neo-Platonists such as Clement of Alexandria, who called Plato the "Moses of Athens," and Origen, a common foil for

---

[34] On Michel de l'Hôpital, see Seong-Hak Kim, *Michel de l'Hôpital: The Vision of a Reformist Chancellor During the French Religious Wars* (Kirksville, MO: Truman State University Press, 1997); Kim, "'Dieu nous garde de la messe du chancelier': The Religious Belief and Political Opinion of Michel de l'Hôpital," *Sixteenth Century Journal* 24, no. 3 (1993): 595–620.

[35] La Place, *Du droict usage*, a6v; *Right Use*, 6.

those who were critical of an excessive use of Plato. He cites Tertullian who said that Plato "spiced the sauce of heresies."[36]

Recognizing that this particular treatise is but a brief introduction to the topic, La Place points out that his goal in writing it is to allow access for a wider audience. So, he attempted to compose the work in a brief and simple style so that it could benefit as many people as possible in the realm. A second goal was to compare classical models of moral philosophy to Christian doctrine and ethics in order to come to a more useful form of ethics. The problem with classical approaches to moral philosophy from Plato to Aristotle to the Epicureans and Stoics is that the entire topic evolved into an academic exercise that La Place labels a kind of "fencing match." It should have been the basis for regulating proper public and private conduct, but it became removed from everyday life.[37]

La Place defines moral philosophy as "nothing but an exposition of the law of nature by which everyone can see with considerable ease, pleasure, and contentment how the precepts and teachings of natural law are naturally imprinted on us, and by which everyone can tame and soften human morals and outward life, which had once been savage and fierce, finding the mean with reason as its compass and rejecting the extremes of excess and deficiency."[38] The ultimate goal of this discipline is to reach the sovereign good, which classically has been defined as the highest good for a state or its people. It consists of happiness, felicity, and beatitude. However, these ends have historically been defined in various ways, and La Place here refers to Marcus Terentius Varro (116–27 BC), the great Roman scholar who, as Augustine recounted, came up with two to three hundred possibilities for the highest good. Epicurus, for example, defined felicity as the pursuit of pleasure and self-preservation as natural to humans. La Place's description of this view is extremely brief, and he spends more time refuting it than describing it. His main objection is that if pleasure were the chief end of man, then animals would share the

---

[36] La Place, *Du droict usage*, 4r–6v; *Right Use*, 13–15.
[37] La Place, *Du droict usage*, 5r–7r; *Right Use*, 14–15.
[38] La Place, *Du droict usage*, 2v–3r; *Right Use*, 12.

same goal. Second, those who primarily seek pleasure at times feel remorse in that accomplishment since some believe that they may have used evil or immoral means. True pleasure, by contrast, consists in following the will of God.[39]

Some seek pleasure in the public realm in the pursuit of glory, esteem, and honor. True honor is derived from one's virtuous acts toward another person, but then the honor is not found in the subject itself but in its object. Aristotle, by contrast, argued that felicity finds its roots both in acts of virtue and in the process of contemplation. One aspect of this process is active and the second more passive. Neither, La Place points out, can be sufficient in and of itself. It is not suitable for one to be entirely contemplative or to live one's life entirely in acts of virtue without spending time thinking and meditating upon those possible actions.[40]

Likewise, La Place deems as deficient Plato's contention that the sovereign good lies in the idea of the good. Plato argued that this concept of good includes a firm knowledge of virtue that inevitably leads to virtuous actions. However, according to La Place, it is difficult to arrive at a sure understanding of the idea of the good. We see only a shadow of it in created things, but our senses sometimes deceive us as we can see only a shadow of reality. While Plato's concept of the good leads to a limited attempt to understand that the ultimate good lies in the knowledge of God, the process fails to understand the limits of the human mind. God is infinite, and we cannot on our own come to understand him. We need to resort to revelation to see that Christ himself leads us in the path of righteous living and shows us the true, sovereign good.[41]

Philosophy is extremely limited in its ability to discover true felicity in comparison to revelation. It sees God only as an angry judge and is ignorant of the true nature of human depravity. Leading one astray, if

---

[39] La Place, *Du droict usage*, 7r–14v; *Right Use*, 16–21.
[40] La Place, *Du droict usage*, 14v–17v; *Right Use*, 21–23.
[41] La Place, *Du droict usage*, 17v–22v; *Right Use*, 23–27.

one is overdependent on it, philosophy results in despair and ignorance and can even lead a person to blaspheme God.[42]

Moral philosophy, however, must not be confused with Christian doctrine. Its focus is limited to proper outward behavior leading to public virtue, while theology focuses on the internal aspects of one's life and reveals the true will of God. Good works in the Christian life flow from the inward, spiritual dimension of one's connection to God. However, even good works that flow from God are, in themselves, imperfect in comparison to God's holiness.[43]

Philosophy is correct in pointing to the soul as the true seat of human felicity because it is the part of humans that comes closest to God. However, La Place contends that humanity's sovereign good must go beyond acts of virtue to acts of a distinctively Christian virtue that point ultimately to God's glory. La Place concludes this section by saying that the glory of God is preferable to all human goods, wealth, and honor. It should be prized above all else, and no person should give it up for "any fear of evil, danger, poverty, exile, torment, and even death itself."[44] This particular statement is extremely poignant since La Place eventually made the ultimate sacrifice during the St. Bartholomew's Day Massacre.

La Place points to what he calls a uniquely Christian form of virtue. Christian virtue, he argues, can be defined as "a habit produced in us by the Holy Spirit, inclining the will to obedience to God." This is contrasted with La Place's summary of Aristotle's definition that virtue "is a habit that inclines one to act according to right reason." The key for La Place is the role of the Holy Spirit and a true change of the heart. Philosophy, by contrast, focuses more on mere external behavior. Pagans, however, can and have performed acts of virtue, mostly because God provided restraint in order to preserve the human race. Furthermore, such virtue cannot be equated with affections since people cannot be called good or evil based solely on their affections, which can change based on circumstances. It is how one responds to

---

[42] La Place, *Du droict usage*, 20v–22r; *Right Use*, 25–26.

[43] La Place, *Du droict usage*, 40v–41v; *Right Use*, 43.

[44] La Place, *Du droict usage*, 24r–v; *Right Use*, 29.

xxxi

difficult circumstances that shows the degree to which one displays virtue.⁴⁵

Moderation serves as an essential aspect of virtue, and here La Place relies upon Aristotle's definition of the mean, distinguishing between arithmetic and geometric means. The latter varies depending on the individual, while the former is simply the middle number equidistant from two extremes. One determines the geometric mean through the use of right reason. Doing good, he points out, is much harder than doing evil. There are many ways to miss the target, but only one way to hit it.⁴⁶

La Place then discusses specific virtues and their intermediate point as well as their extremes. For example, in his evaluation of the virtue of strength, he notes the extremes of rashness and audacity on the one hand and fear and cowardliness on the other. Another virtue would be generosity, and the extremes would be avarice and lavishness. He lists other virtues in a similar way. The trick to acting in a virtuous manner is constant evaluation, and if one errs, it should be in the direction of the lesser evil.⁴⁷

He rejects the views of the Stoics, who diminished affections such as concupiscence, joy, and fear, and favors the view of the Peripatetics who argued that such dispositions are innate to mankind. They can be controlled and moderated but not eliminated.⁴⁸

La Place carefully slips some aspects of Reformed doctrine into the treatise and condemns the semi-Pelagian notion that humans can do good works pleasing to God in a state of nature. He directly refutes the late-medieval notion that if human beings do the best they can do, God will infallibly reward them with grace as a just due. He makes an important distinction between works performed in domestic, civil, and political affairs and those done in spiritual matters. The former can be considered just and wise from the perspective of one's fellow

---

[45] La Place, *Du droict usage*, 72v–74r; *Right Use*, 69–70.

[46] La Place, *Du droict usage*, 68v–72v; *Right Use*, 66–68.

[47] La Place, *Du droict usage*, 76r–84v; *Right Use*, 71–78.

[48] La Place, *Du droict usage*, 84r–86r; *Right Use*, 78–80.

human beings and can, in a sense, serve as a form of public justification. However, good works performed in ecclesiastical or spiritual affairs cannot meet God's perfect standards and, therefore, fail to provide ultimate justification. Ultimately one must rely upon God for the ability to obey his moral law. If one could obey the moral law in a state of nature, then Christ died for nothing.[49]

La Place concludes his discussion of moral virtue with some advice for public officials, such as Michel de l'Hôpital, who should give glory to Jesus Christ in their actions and rely on God's strength to carry out the laws of the land in a just and virtuous way.[50] Unfortunately for La Place, not all French magistrates heeded his advice.

---

[49] La Place, *Du droict usage*, 60r–64r, 93v–97r, 99v–101r; *Right Use*, 57–60, 86–88, 90–91.

[50] La Place, *Du droict usage*, 99v–101r; *Right Use*, 90–91.

xxxiii

Bibliography

Buchon, J. A. C. *Choix de chroniques et mémoires sur l'histoire de France, avec notices biographiques.* Paris: A. Desrez, 1836.

Buisson, Albert. *Michel de l'Hospital, 1503-1573.* Paris: Hachette, 1950.

Cabanel, Patrick. *Histoire des protestants en France XVIe-XXIe siècle.* Paris: Fayard, 2012.

Daussy, Hugues. *Le Parti Huguenot: Chronique d'une désillusion (1557-1572).* Geneva: Droz, 2015.

Gilmont, Jean-François. "Les premières éditions des ouvrages de La Place et de La Popelinère." *Revue française d'histore du livre* 55 (1986): 119-52.

Haag, Eugène, and Émile Haag. *La France Protestante: ou vies des protestants français qui se sont fait un nom dans l'Histoire depuis les premiers temps de la réformation jusqu'à la reconnaissance du principe de la liberté des cultes par l'assemblée nationale.* Vol. 6, *Huber-Lesage.* Paris: Joël Cherbuliez, 1857.

Holt, Mack P. *The French Wars of Religion, 1562-1629.* 2nd ed. Cambridge: Cambridge University Press, 2005.

Kess, Alexandra. *Johann Sleidan and the Protestant Vision of History.* Farnham, UK: Ashgate, 2008.

Kim, Seong-Hak. "'Dieu nous garde de la messe du chancelier': The Religious Belief and Political Opinion of Michel de l'Hôpital." *The Sixteenth Century Journal* 24, no. 3 (1993): 595-620.

———. *Michel de l'Hôpital: The Vision of a Reformist Chancellor During the French Religious Wars.* Kirksville, MO: Truman State University Press, 1997.

Kingdon, Robert M. *Myths about the St. Bartholomew's Day Massacres, 1572-1576.* Cambridge, MA: Harvard University Press, 1988.

Knecht, R. J. *The French Wars of Religion, 1559-1698.* 3rd ed. London: Routledge, 2010.

La Place, Pierre de. *Commentaires de l'estat de la religion et république sous les rois Henry & François seconds, & Charles neuvième.* N.p.: n.p., 1565. Latin translation: *Commentariorum de statu religionis & reipublicæ in regno*

INTRODUCTION

Galliæ I. partis libri III. Regibus Henrico secundo ... Francisco secundo, & Carolo nono. Recogniti & plerisque in locis emendati (n.p.: n.p., 1572–75). English translation: *The fyrst parte of commentaries, concerning the state of religion, and the common wealthe of Fraunce, under the reignes of Henry the second, Frauncis the second, and Charles the ninth*. Translated by Thomas Tymme. London: Henrie Bynneman, 1573.

———. *Du droict usage de la philosophie morale avec la doctrine chrestienne*. Paris: Morel, 1562.

———. *Paraphrasis in titulos institutionum imperialium de actionibus, exceptionibus et interdictis Scholiis seorsum margini appositis*. Paris: Galiot du Pré, 1546.

———. *Traicté de l'excellence de l'homme chrestien et manière de le cognoistre*. [Geneva]: [Jacob Stoer], 1575. English translation: *A treatise of the excellencie of a christian man, and how he may be knowen*. Translated by Laurence Tomson. London: Christopher Barker, 1576.

———. *Traitté de la vocation et maniere de vivre a laquelle chacun est appellé*. Paris: Morel, 1561. English translation: *Politique discourses: treating of the differences and inequalities of vocation, as well publique as private: with the scopes or endes whereunto they are directed*. Translated by Ægremont Ratcliffe. London: Edward Aggas, 1578. Latin translation: *De vocatione, seu de ea vivendi ratione ad quam quisque vocatus est, libri tres*. In Pierre de la Place, *Petri Plateani viri clarissimi, in curia parisiensi regiorum subsidiorum, seu vectigalium praesidis primatii, Opuscula* [...], 109–247. [Geneva]: Eustathius Vignon, 1587.

Sleidanus, Johannes. *De statu religionis et reipublicae, Carolo Quinto, Caesare, commentarii*. 2 vols. [Strasbourg]: Rihelius, 1555.

Strohm, Christoph. *Ethik im frühen Calvinismus: Humanistische Einflüsse, philosophische, juristische und theologische Argumentationen sowie mentalitätsgeschichtliche Aspekte am Beispiel des Calvin-Schülers Lambertus Danaeus*. Berlin: W. de Gruyter, 1996.

White, Henry. *The Massacre of St. Bartholomew: Preceded by a History of the Religious Wars in the Reign of Charles IX*. New York: Harper, 1868.

Yardeni, Myriam. *Minorités et mentalités religieuses en Europe moderne: L'Exemple des Huguenots*. Edited by Michael Green. Paris: Honoré Champion, 2018.

---. "La pensée politique de la première historiographie huguenote: Pierre de la Place et Louis Régnier de La Planche." In *Cité des hommes, cité de Dieu. Travaux sur la littérature de la Renaissance en l'honneur de Daniel Ménager*, edited by Jean Céard, Marie-Christine Gomez-Géraud, Michel Magnien, and François Rouget, 101–10. Geneva: Droz, 2003.

The Right Use of
Moral Philosophy

Epistle

To Monseigneur the Chancellor of France,
Lord Michel de l'Hôpital.

I do not doubt, Monseigneur, that the title of this book alone will already be offensive to some. For they think that a statesman active in the exercise of justice ought not to involve himself in or touch upon anything related to the theological profession, which in their eyes is remote and distant, or even altogether different from politics, with its boundaries and reach extending beyond the science of civil and political laws, constitutions, and statutes within which they want to confine politics. They think the same of anyone who, so they say, fails to restrict each and every vocation within its limits, since they would not have one encroach upon the other. And so I foresee that they will not fail to say of me what was said of Cleon in Aristophanes, namely, that I have one foot in the city and the other in the field[1]—that is, that I am leaving my profession and intruding upon and applying myself to another that is not mine. But, Monseigneur, such men I want to satisfy first and foremost of my ability, and to cause them to better understand my intention, which they cannot know. For I am not one to mix what belongs to one vocation with another in any way, since I find such confusion more horrifying than anything else. Even less am I among those who seek to go beyond their own vocation and to take up what is not theirs. But I want everyone to understand how their view, which

---

[1] Aristophanes, *Knights*, lines 75–76.

is widespread today, comes only from ignorance and from a failure to understand properly what belongs to the exercise of justice and in what that exercise truly consists. For there is no doubt that the exercise of justice consists above all in the inquiry and true knowledge of what is just and unjust, and consequently as much—or even more—in the science of the divine as in the human.[2] Natural law, from which civil laws and constitutions are derived, is only a very small part of the divine law, and in many things it remains degraded and corrupted by human malice, so that the principal reason for the establishment of the magistracy has been deemed to be nothing other than the complete maintenance of the two tables of God's law. It follows from this that there is no vocation that has greater need of being fashioned after the rule of Holy Scripture, and consequently that none has greater need of the knowledge it contains. The gentiles and pagans duly recognized that the philosophy treating of human morals, tasks, and duties belongs to and is necessary for this profession, serving it in the exposition of the law of nature. Will we then say that theology, which is proper to and intended for the interpretation of God's law, itself the light of and science for all other laws, does not have anything to do with it? Indeed, in antiquity philosophers and lawyers came from one and the same school, and were taught by the same master and preceptor. We read this of Panaetius and Rutilius, for example, the former a philosopher and the latter a lawyer, who were auditors and students together under the philosopher Diogenes the Stoic. So too after them the philosopher Hecaton and the lawyer Tubero studied together under this same Panaetius, and so the list goes on.[3] The alliance and link between these two sciences is known to be such that to disjoin and separate them would end up spoiling them both, rendering the one as well as the other lacking and imperfect. This is why Cicero says that the science of laws is not to be sought in the edicts of preceptors or even in

---

[2] See Digest 1.1.10.2, in Theodore Mommsen, ed., *Corpus Iuris Civilis*, vol. 1, *Digesta*, editio stereotypa sexta (Berlin: Weidmann, 1893), 1.

[3] Rutilius (Publius Rutilius Rufus) (b. 160 BC) was not a student of Diogenes, but of Panaetius (ca. 185–109 BC). Hecaton and Tubero were also students of Panaetius.

the laws of the Twelve Tables, but that one must dig down to the deepest depths of philosophy.[4] We likewise, and with greater reason, shall say that theology ought to be joined and united with the civil and political science, and that the true science of laws ought to lean on Scripture as its true source and origin. And if, therefore, this science is born of and comes from the divine law, and must be regulated according to it, what will become of it if its only guide and light is the vanity of the reasoning of the human mind, filled as it is with ignorance and blindness? Will it suffice to see a judge seated on the sacred seat of justice, instructed by barbarian and pagan laws alone, and will he so exercise a justice that is not human but divine, making unwavering pronouncements on the life of people with respect to faith and their relationships with others? The ancients considered the man of justice who was ignorant of philosophy to be unworthy of his name. Will we, then, say that the profane—that is, those who are ignorant of Scripture—are worthy of that title? Aristotle lamented his time, when men of the legal profession were ignorant of philosophy. But is there any less occasion to complain at the present time, when we see them ignorant not only in moral and political philosophy, but also—and this is worse!—in Scripture and theology, since they have been taught the vain and foolish view that Scripture and theology have nothing to teach them? The erudite are well aware that they face the examples of countless great men including Justin Martyr, Tertullian, Athanasius, Saint Ambrose, Nectarius, Pope Gregory, Chrysostom, and countless others in a list too long to recite. All of them were lawyer-theologians, and most of them were also drawn and called from political life into the ecclesiastical state. I am well aware that if we consider the exercise and ministry of one of these two professions, we will quickly find that they are two totally distinct and separate vocations, which ought not to be confused in any way. But here we are speaking about the sciences of these two professions, and we say that they ought not to be disjoined; rather, the civil science must be aided by the divine and take from the latter what it itself lacks. For if things had gone that way up to the present time, we would not have fallen into the labyrinth of lawsuits

---

[4] Cicero, *On the Laws* 1.5.17.

in which we currently find ourselves in this kingdom: its three estates have virtually been changed and converted into a single estate of people who plead their cause at one moment and render judgment at another[5]—a state of affairs that I can only attribute first and foremost to the ignorance of Scripture and to the nonchalant treatment of it. From that ignorance necessarily follow all errors and obscurities, and consequently all trouble, discord, and contention. For without the light of Scripture human life is like a dangerous crossing during a dark and cloudy night. It is thus sufficiently clear that theology is required for and necessary to the civil and political science, and even incomparably more so to philosophy, especially since it cannot as much as indicate the true goal and end at which the political man must aim all his actions and fashion them accordingly. This makes it very clear that both philosophy and the science of laws, each on its own (i.e., either one of them without theology), is lacking and imperfect. And, just as we have said that philosophy alone is imperfect, so too we must admit that when it is mixed together with theology, philosophy is dangerous and greatly to be feared. This is why Tertullian called it the very sauce and seasoning of heresies.[6] Yet the difficult thing is to know how the two might be properly distinguished, and above all how philosophy might be kept strictly within its limits. This is, in short, the true way to learn how to use philosophy properly, or how to make both philosophy and theology useful and profitable. I had given frequent consideration to this matter, Monseigneur, and at times even considered writing about it, waiting for some respite from my constant

---

[5] Beyond the monarchy, medieval French society was ordered into three estates: the first, clergy; the second, nobility; and the third, the bourgeoisie and peasants (or, those who prayed, those who fought, and those who worked). This *ancien régime* was in effect until the revolution in the eighteenth century. See Gail Bossenga, "Society," in *Old Regime France, 1648–1788*, ed. William Doyle (Oxford: Oxford University Press, 2001), 42–77. Cf. Georges Duby, *The Three Orders: Feudal Society Imagined*, trans. Arthur Goldhammer (Chicago: University of Chicago Press, 1980); P. S. Lewis, *Later Medieval France: The Polity* (London: Macmillan, 1968).

[6] Tertullian, *On the Soul* 23.5.

service to the people, when misfortune presented me with an occasion, as the opportune rest I needed, to satisfy this desire. I am referring to the threat of the plague that recently came over us here, so that I withdrew to the countryside, where I saw that I could not serve the public any better way than by writing. And so I applied myself to the study of this topic, namely how moral philosophy might be used rightly and properly with Christian doctrine, while exposing the danger that follows from the confusion of the two. I leave it up to others to judge the fruit of my labor. Nevertheless, I can assure everyone that it was written with the intention of being profitable, even making common and familiar knowledge of what has up to now been the province of only a few. When, at the end, I considered to whom I might best present this labor of mine, I found that what pertains to morality and is closely related to religious matters—treating of the moral, civil, and Christian virtues and pertaining to the civil, political, and Christian man—could not be better dedicated than to one in whom all these sorts of virtues are best imprinted and unified, or by whom they have been better grasped and understood, and who currently deploys them and puts them to work and displays them to the exceptional profit of all during these troubling times. Your deliberations and actions, Monseigneur, are known to be such that they all tend to the extirpation and uprooting of avarice, ambition, excess, and superstition, and planting equity, justice, sincerity, and purity of religion in their stead. As you might well imagine, there will be plenty of grievances and complaints, in many different ways. But you also know how in times of tempest the wise pilot, attentive to the passage of his vessel, does not stop at the shouts and cries of his passengers, and how the surgeon, confident and experienced in his art, does not stop at the cries and tears of a patient when he is resetting a disjointed limb. Therefore, the only thing that now remains for me to do, Monseigneur, is to beg you to receive this small labor of mine in favor, looking not so much at the value of this gift as at the devotion of him who humbly offers it to you. My desire is to remain in your good graces, and to serve you humbly. I pray God that he will prosper you in the administration and charge committed to you, and may assist, guide, and direct your actions to his glory and to the rest and tranquility of the republic.

Book One

Book One

1. The excellence of the science of morals over all human sciences.

Among all the arts and sciences devised by human reason, that in which the art of living well consists—ethics, that is, morals—can rightly be considered the most profitable and necessary of all. This is because it treats of human morals and the way to cultivate them well, and it makes the human mind ready and renders it better disposed and prepared to receive the seed of civil and political virtues, and to live in closer unity. For ethics is what gathered the scattered people together, first in houses and families, then in villages, burgs, towns, and cities, and finally in provinces, kingdoms, and empires. It also gave them their laws, magistrates, and institution to bring and keep them together in a single body and community. Therefore, whether we consider a person alone and on his own, or in his family and household, or even in the political assembly, we will always find this science to be the true guide for human life, the director of virtues, and the teacher of all good morals and discipline. Accordingly, it was not without good reason that Plato said that this science is a gift and blessing from the gods, sent from heaven to the human race here on earth.[1] It truly is an inestimable treasure with which God sought to enrich even the infidels and pagans, not only to preserve the association

---

[1] See Plato, *Meno* 99e4.

among men and to keep them united and allied, but also to lead them by this means into knowledge of his divinity.

For, aside from reforming morals and producing the laws and institutions of republics, ethics gives us a clearer witness of God's light in that the immutable and eternal difference between what is good and upright versus what is evil and dishonorable, which the doctrine of morals teaches us, testifies sufficiently that human nature was not made randomly, as some have thought, but by a sovereign power and divine providence. Consequently, this difference between what is good and evil shows us that God is just, wise, and true, perfect and without any deficiency in goodness and virtue. It furthermore incites us to consider what even Cicero says, namely that the first association people have is with God; to reflect even more fully and closely on our being, so that we might go so far as to feel the rays of God's wisdom and virtue shining in us; and, finally, to know that man, by an admirable counsel of God, was created in his image, that is to say, created in such a way that God's goodness, wisdom, and other virtues might shine in us and be made known there.[2]

Moral philosophy is, properly speaking, nothing but an exposition of the law of nature by which everyone can see with considerable ease, pleasure, and contentment how the precepts and teachings of natural law are naturally imprinted on us, and by which everyone can tame and soften human morals and outward life, which had once been savage and fierce, finding the mean with reason as its compass and rejecting the extremes of excess and deficiency. Moral philosophy has explained and deployed these virtues so familiarly and captured their natural beauty in such a lifelike manner that no one fails to be incited by it to love these virtues all the more. For by its very nature virtue has the capacity to affect anyone as soon as he knows it, so that he suddenly finds virtue's acts to be beautiful and seeks to shape his life by their mold. In fact, no one fails to realize that he has been taught sufficiently by this science to discern how far natural reason can guide and lead us in judging the morals, lives, and acts of our fellow human

---

[2] Cicero, *On the Laws* 1.8.25.

beings. It should, therefore, be clear that we ought not to admit the view of those who outright reject and trample upon the moral teaching of the ancient philosophers as if it were a withered and worthless remnant from the past. For when we look at their moral teaching, we clearly see the contrary, and even see the generosity God showed to the pagans of old when he invited them to know him by this means and an infinite number of others such that they are without any excuse before his judgment.[3]

2. The bad that results from the confusion of the science of morals with Christian doctrine; and how the Epicureans, sophists, and scholastics, and even the first and most ancient church fathers, have misused it.

Yet for all our disagreement with those who reject the moral teaching of the ancients wholesale, we also cannot but condemn others who confuse that ancient teaching with theology, extending it too far, namely, beyond what concerns civil life and human society. For it is no small error to view moral philosophy and Christian doctrine as one and the same thing. Moral philosophy is limited to certain precepts and teachings for outward action, and seeks to accustom and habituate people to them, so that it might lead them to a civil and political virtue, adorning and clothing them on the outside with a visible act, and looking for no more than an external and human righteousness. Christian doctrine, on the other hand, goes much further, unveils the will of God, and teaches us whatever belongs to a righteousness that is internal, spiritual, and divine, from which good works flow as from their proper source, even though God cannot receive them as pleasing to him in spite of the beauty with which they are adorned.

All that Plato taught here and there relating to moral philosophy, which he had learned from the instruction of his teacher Socrates, Aristotle reduced to a single work with a singular order and disposition,[4] skillfully making a complete body out of the various members

---

[3] Cf. Rom. 1:20.

[4] I.e., *Nicomachean Ethics*.

that had formerly been scattered. Some who came after him, such as the Epicureans and Stoics, by their zeal for controversy more than anything else (or so it seems), followed trivialities and frivolous conjectures rather than certain demonstrations, and thus arrived at another form of teaching. Yet others who came after them thought they were shedding light on this philosophy (which in itself is suited to all people, and approaches common sense), but actually treated it with shrewd and subtle, sophistic ways of disputation and argumentation. Their intention therefore seemed to have been to withdraw and remove moral philosophy from people's sight and knowledge, rather than to make it more accessible to them. In the end, these philosophers reduced the subject of moral philosophy so far that, instead of serving to shape and establish human morals as it ought to have, it seemed to be no more than a fencing match (so to speak) and a pastime for men who spent their time uselessly at school without gaining any profit from it. Even worse, this way of disputing and arguing came to be so highly regarded that people were no longer content merely to have it adapted to the science of morals in this useless fashion, but also began to apply it to Scripture, mixing philosophy and theology—that is, heaven and earth—with such error and confusion that we need not look any further for the cause of all heresies and false doctrines that have ever arisen down to our very own time. For we have to admit that from the very beginning, immediately after the time of the apostles, the church's early and leading doctors, who came from the school of Plato in which they had been raised, deferred to philosophy much more often than they ought to have. When Justin Martyr joined the Christian church, he did not want to give up his philosopher's cloak, holding that Plato's teaching agreed with the gospel.[5] Around the same time Clement of Alexandria, the preceptor of Origen, called Plato the Moses of Athens,[6] and on the same account Arnobius called him the

---

[5] See Justin Martyr, *First Apology* 44, 59–60; *Dialogue with Trypho* 2–3.

[6] Clement of Alexandria, *Stromata* 1.22.150 (citing Numenius); see also Eusebius, *Preparation for the Gospel* 11.10.14.

Christian Philosopher.[7] Here and there we read Porphyry reproaching Origen for having once had the custom of always holding Plato in hand, but then abandoning him for Christian doctrine.[8] Oh that his reproach were true! For the reading of Origen's books easily leads us to the contrary conclusion. I therefore think Tertullian stated it well when he said that it is Plato who has spiced the sauce of heresies.[9] And what likeness is there, he says, between the philosopher and the Christian, between the disciple of Greece and the disciple of heaven, between an enemy and the friend of error, and between the one who dresses up the truth and another who squeezes out true sap from it?[10] And yet Tertullian himself was unable to do more than skirt its temptations. It was thus not without reason that Saint Paul admonished the Colossians so ardently to watch that they not be taken captive by philosophy and empty deceit according to the traditions and institutions of men, and not according to Jesus Christ.[11]

Since it was our design to provide a brief exposition of what belongs to moral philosophy, we decided first to accommodate ourselves to the subject matter as much as possible, and in doing so to treat and write of it most simply, in a straightforward and common style. This is to make it accessible to each and every person's mind, rendering it more popular, common, and familiar than it has ever been before. We also resolved to compare this philosophy with Christian doctrine in order to present their respective ends, as well as the difference between them, so as to make them both more useful and profitable.

---

[7] Cf. Eusebius, *Preparation for the Gospel* 13.12.1–4. Arnobius was a teacher of rhetoric who died in the fourth century AD.

[8] See Eusebius, *Ecclesiastical History* 6.19.5–9. Porphyry (AD 234–ca. 305) was a student of the philosopher Plotinus. He wrote on religion and philosophy, including commentaries on works of Plato and Aristotle.

[9] Tertullian, *On the Soul* 23.5.

[10] Tertullian, *On the Prescription against Heretics* 7.

[11] Col. 2:8.

3. All human actions and deliberations have an end; the diversity of ends, and how the remotest end is the most excellent and that in which the sovereign good resides.

To begin our brief treatment of moral philosophy: it is certain that, just as those who undertake a trip normally have some goal or destination in mind as the end of their voyage to which they guide and adjust their entire route and travels, so too there is no human deliberation, undertaking, or act that does not have an end proposed and destined as its good. Since people naturally apply themselves to what they think ought to be good for them (differing in this from brute animals which, being destitute of reason and driven by natural instinct alone to what is present to them without any concern for the future, have no end proposed to their act), they always set a goal for their acts, driven as they are by the guidance of reason. This is why the ancients, when they offered a brief definition of the good, said that it is what all things long for and desire for their good, being aware of man's natural inclination to focus uniquely on what he deems to be good. For just as it is natural for the eye to seek light, so the natural inclination of the human will is to desire and want what seems good to it.

Furthermore, just as human acts are diverse, so too are the ends, with some ends being more excellent than others. For the military art has its acts and its end (i.e., victory), which is more excellent than the end of the art of architecture (i.e., a building). Similarly, the end of the art of medicine, which is health, is to be esteemed more highly than the end of a tailor or shoemaker, which is a dress and a shoe, and so on. Each end proposed to the human mind has other first and second ends, serving as degrees and means by which one arrives at it. So, in order to achieve victory, which is the end of the military art, there are other ends such as the art of brandishing arms, then the art of waging war, and several other ends. From this it follows that the more distant and remote the end, the more worthy and excellent it is, until from one end to the other one gradually arrives at the last and final end of all, which alone is to be loved and taken hold of for its own regard and sake, rather than for the sake of others. That is what sets it apart from all the others, since the latter are all loved and desired not

Book One

for their own sake, but for the sake of the last end to which all others look as the one in which the sovereign good[12] over them all consists.

4. The order for arriving at knowledge of the sovereign good, and what those who want to be students of the science of morals ought to be like.

For to think that there is no fixed end to all human acts in which this sovereign good can be found would be to accuse nature falsely of an infinite confusion, or even to deny that the minds of all men have this common, proper, and natural desire to reach a final point, which we then cannot find. This is the first point we wish to make for all who desire to be well instructed in life and its morals, so that they can better guide their works and acts with this goal fixed before their eyes—just as the archer shoots his arrow more accurately when he aims at the target, than he would otherwise.[13] But if we could see the excellent beauty and perfection of this sovereign good with our eyes, how much more would our hearts be kindled and enflamed to love it ardently and to pursue it unfailingly?

We have therefore come to know in quick order that there is a sovereign good over all things, to which all others relate. And we arrived at this knowledge by the consideration of human acts and their end (following here the order maintained by the philosophers), which are closer, more familiar, and better known to us, passing more easily from them to knowledge of the things that are more distant from us and less well known than we would have if we had taken the opposite route and starting point of the things that are less well known to us and more remote, working our way down to those that are closer and more easily and readily reached. As such we have not followed the order of nature,

---

[12] *souuerain bien*. The Latin translation renders this as *summum bonum*. Pierre de la Place, *De recto usu moralis philosophiae cum doctrina Christiana collatae, libri tres*, in *Petri Plateani viri clarissimi, in curia parisiensi regiorum subsidiorum, seu vectigalium praesidis primatii, Opuscula* [...] ([Geneva]: Eustathius Vignon, 1587), 8.

[13] Cf. Aristotle, *Nicomachean Ethics* 1.2 (1094a23–24).

where the causes and principles of each thing are known before the effects that follow from them. Yet in this we accommodate ourselves to the frailty and weakness of the mind, which gains knowledge of the effects (i.e., our acts) more easily than it does of the perfect good (i.e., the cause from which our acts proceed). We see this from experience in the case of a lunar eclipse, which we know more quickly than its cause, which is the earth's position between the moon and the sun. There are many other easy examples of a similar nature.

Aristotle says that those who want to grasp this moral science well must first have some experience with good morals and be accustomed to doing good, so that thereafter they can better understand that there is a final end in which this sovereign good of which we are speaking resides, adding that it is otherwise difficult to listen to this science and doctrine. And just as it is said of those who want to understand the mathematical sciences well that they must first have some principles and foundations from themselves (e.g., that the sum is greater than a part), as well as other principles shown to them by their teacher (e.g., that two equidistant lines, which are called parallels, never come together)—so anyone who wants to become a good student of the science of morality must first have some rudiments of doing well that he himself has gained by experience, as well as a number of other foundations that he has from the mouth of his master, by which he can more easily know that there is a sovereign good to which all actions aspire. "Otherwise," so Aristotle says, "anyone who has no foundation of his own, nor even the intention of getting it from others, must hear what the poet Hesiod has to say on this:

> Far best is he who knows all things himself;
> Good, he that hearkens when men counsel right;
> But he who neither knows, nor lays to heart
> Another's wisdom, is a useless wight."[14]

---

[14] Aristotle, *Nicomachean Ethics* 1.4 (1095a31–b13), quoting Hesiod, *Works and Days*, lines 293–97. English translation from W. D. Ross, trans., *Nicomachean Ethics*, in *The Complete Works of Aristotle*, ed. Jonathan Barnes, 2 vols. (Princeton: Princeton University Press, 1984), 2:1731.

5. The excellence of the sovereign good is more apparent in the science of politics, and also more necessary for it than for all other sciences.

We have thus found that there is a sovereign good over all things and learned that this sovereign good is so important that on its knowledge depends the principle guide and director for our works and acts, which is the true goal of this life at which everyone must aim. There is no doubt that, among all sciences and acts, the sovereign good presents its excellence best in that which is called the civil and political science. This science is superior because it commands all sciences and acts and because they all accommodate themselves to it, tending to one and the same end in which they are all comprised.[15] It is very clear that this sovereign good, which is proposed to all sciences and acts, shows and presents itself more excellently there than anywhere else—it is just as clear, in fact, as when we see that although light and brightness is always one (whether it enlightens one, or several things, or all), nevertheless it appears incomparably more excellent and admirable when it shines on all than when it shines on only a few. From this it follows that the knowledge of the sovereign good of which we are speaking is much more necessary to the science of politics and political activity than it is to all other sciences, since the former extends universally to the conduct and principal administration of all men.

6. The sovereign good is called felicity, and what true felicity is.

Now, however, it is time to consider and look most closely at what this sovereign good is. To begin with its name, there has been little difficulty in this regard, since all have called it "destiny," "felicity," and "beatitude."[16] The real difficulty lies in knowing what this felicity is, and in what it consists. To avoid reciting the many diverse opinions, of

---

[15] Cf. Aristotle, *Nicomachean Ethics* 1.2 (1094a18–b11); *Politics* 1.1 (1252a1–6).

[16] *heur, felicité, beatitude.*

which Varro managed to list two to three hundred different kinds,[17] since everyone proposes his own respective end and felicity according to the way of living that seems most agreeable to him, we will list only three main ways of living wherein felicity is defined differently.[18]

7. The felicity of the life of pleasure, and Epicurus's view of it.

The first is that which follows a person's wishes and whims, and its final end is pleasure. This way of living attracts and kindles the majority of people as if it were nature's most certain and fixed end. Epicurus, who was the originator and first proponent of this view, says that the end of nature is that to which it is most inclined and most voluntarily driven of its own accord, without any outside constraint. And so we say that what is natural for a stone is to go down, and not to go up, because it is voluntary (so to speak) with respect to the former, but forced and constrained from the outside with respect to the latter. Since, therefore, human nature tends to this end of a person's wish and pleasure, it follows that pleasure as the final end of nature is that in which the real point of felicity consists. Epicurus adds that the natural appetite that is best ordered and proper to itself is that which tends first of all to self-preservation, and that, just as displeasure tends first of all to a person's ruin and destruction, so their delight and pleasure tend rather to a person's preservation. And, consequently, for Epicurus true felicity is pleasure.

This view, however, is altogether false, uncultivated, and repugnant to reason. For if indeed our end were pleasure, it would follow that brute animals participate in the same felicity as us, since we share with them the sensitive part in which the proponents of this view constitute

---

[17] Marcus Terentius Varro (116–27 BC) was one of the greatest scholars of Roman antiquity, but only two of his many works survive in any substantial form. Varro's list of opinions about the highest good, and the philosophical sects corresponding to these opinions, is discussed at length in Augustine, *City of God* 19.1–3.

[18] For the three main ways of living and their respective accounts of the highest good, see Aristotle, *Nicomachean Ethics* 1.5 (1095b14–1096a5).

their felicity. Moreover, to say that a person's natural inclination is of itself ready to follow pleasure and forced to follow what is virtuous is insufficient to locate the sovereign good there, since pleasure-seekers in all their delights and pleasures do feel pangs of remorse, convincing them that there is evil in their pleasure. Some revulsion therefore marches ahead of the pleasure of sin, closely followed by the stings and stabs that are the prompt executors of divine justice—which battle only comes from the disruption in the harmony that had once been in us before sin arrived. Nor is it useful to say that pleasure tends to our preservation, and displeasure to its contrary. For the truth is that when pleasure and displeasure are regulated as they ought to be, they truly tend to the preservation of the state of nature. But this is not pleasure as Epicurus understood it, but the pleasure for which human nature was made and created in accordance and conformity with the ordinance of God; when pleasure and displeasure are understood in any other sense, they are nothing but the ruin and destruction of nature.

8. The felicity of political life.

The second way of living is found among those who, having been better instructed and taught, devote themselves to the handling of cases and the management of public affairs. They locate their end in a part of man that is truly better than the sensual part, constituting their felicity in honor, glory, esteem, and reputation, following the example of numerous great and renowned men who knew that honor is so effective that it re-presents the absent, makes the dead alive, and rewards the brevity of this life with a long and happy memory.

The truth of the matter is, however, that they stop at an end that is much more distant and remote than the one we are looking for. For according to their view, honor resides more in the one who acts honorably toward another person than in the one who receives it, so that in order for this view to remain true, it would follow that honor—and thus felicity—is not in the one who is held to be happy but in another. Yet the good of the felicity of which we want to speak is such that it is proper to the one who has it, and is desired only for its own consideration, and not for the sake of another as is the case with honor. For people desire honor not so much to stop at it as they do to acquire a reputation of being virtuous, since those who pursue honor want to be known and honored only for this end of virtue, so that honor is here not the final end, but rather serves as a springboard for another, more distant and better end. Moreover, to fix honor in us as a final end would be to establish an end of vice that is worthy of condemnation.

9. Aristotle's view of felicity.

We now come to the third and final way of living, to see whether we will find there the end disposed for itself rather than for another, in which end perfect felicity resides. Aristotle locates two types of felicity in man: the one in acts of virtue, since virtue on its own, as he says, is a deficiency and useless when it is not exercised by works; and the other in the good received by contemplation.[19] As such he divides people into two parts, namely, an active part and a contemplative part, and therefore creates a division of and separation between virtues, calling the one category intellectual and the other moral[20]—the former being proper to the human mind and intellect, and the latter to people's morals and acts. Yet if we want to retain what we have said above, there cannot be more than a single final end in which the perfect good is and consists, just as we cannot understand how there might be two equally perfect and final ends once it has been established that there is a single sovereign good over all, to be loved for itself and not another, which all others serve and to which they are inferior. The sovereign good therefore cannot belong to human acts alone any more than it can be proper to contemplation alone. For it is difficult to find a person who enjoys the active felicity described by Aristotle—someone, that is, who is accomplished in all virtues, has lived a full and complete human life with riches, health, beauty, strength, and the other graces necessary, as he says, for the exercise of virtue, without any disruption, calamity, or misery of at least some

---

[19] Aristotle, *Nicomachean Ethics* 10.7 (1177a12–22).

[20] Aristotle, *Nicomachean Ethics* 1.13 (1102a27–1103a6).

magnitude. The same thing applies to Aristotle's contemplative felicity, since it is no less difficult to find a spiritual man who does not exercise any corporeal acts, living on contemplation alone, in perpetual search of the occult and secret in nature, and in contemplation of the celestial and divine, not receiving anything except by speculation alone. Elsewhere, in our book on vocation,[21] we showed sufficiently how the contemplative life and the active life are not to be separated from each other in any way, and how everyone ought to participate in both. Since, therefore, intelligible and contemplative virtue cannot come from external action any more than external action can arise from the internal, so too Aristotle's speculation can never bring true and perfect felicity. Nevertheless, for our present purposes we will adopt Aristotle's felicity as if it had not been his intention to cross the boundaries of moral philosophy, which does not extend beyond the action and tranquility of the civil and political life. Since he looked no higher, he constituted the felicity of civil life in the operation of virtue, which properly speaking is virtue itself—although he restricted it to the operation and external exercise of virtue, without extending it to speculation and contemplation.

10. Plato's view of felicity.

But to consider true felicity even more closely, Plato, who went beyond the aforementioned simple consideration of the moral and active, located the sovereign good of man, and thus his felicity, in the Idea of the good (that is, in the immutable, certain, and firm knowledge of virtue, which elicits and guides good works and acts), and he called this Idea eternal, permanent, and immutable, since it resides in demonstrations and in certain, conclusive, and infallible proofs, and since it provides clear insight into the very interior of the thing that is known and always shows the same effects. As such, one cannot be deceived or led astray by this knowledge of the Idea, whereas this does happen with common and everyday knowledge since it does not represent

---

[21] Pierre de la Place, *Traitté de la vocation et manière de vivre à laquelle chacun est appelé* (Paris: Morel, 1561).

things as they really are but only their shadow, so that such false and untrue knowledge must also deceive people in their acts and life.[22] For just as someone who does not have in his mind an image and figure of a building to imitate cannot be a good architect or draw buildings well, and just as someone who does not have some knowledge of war presented to his eyes in all his deliberations cannot be a good captain, so too someone who does not have some knowledge of virtue to follow in all his works and undertakings cannot live uprightly and in the way that is fitting. And it is this perfect knowledge that Plato calls Idea, and in it he constitutes felicity.

11. The most common view among philosophers concerning human felicity, and true felicity according to Christian doctrine.

And although Plato's view does not seem all that far from Aristotle's two kinds of felicity when combined, the latter nevertheless sought to contradict and contest Plato's position in every way. To my mind he did this not so much out of a desire to disprove its truth, but because he held a grudge against this lofty and newfangled way of speaking of Ideas, debating and opposing it in numerous places. Whatever the case may be, since the above view only states that virtue is that in which felicity resides, the philosophers were very keen to follow it, and like Plato they took the term "virtue" to include understanding and knowledge of God, as well as the works performed by that knowledge. These philosophers entered this knowledge of God by way of created things that were joined and united together and were interdependent, and along this ladder the philosophers ascended up into heaven from where they saw that the earth below is governed from heaven with its continual and uniform movement, and that the virtue by which heaven receives its movement is therefore not material or corporeal but spiritual. And so, ascending step by step to some of that lofty knowledge of God as the moving and first cause of all others, they came to recognize—to the degree that the corruption of their nature and their ignorance would allow it—the excellence of his

---

[22] See Plato, *Republic* 7.514a–20a.

beauty from the beauty of created things, his infinite wisdom from creation's order and harmony, and invisible works from visible works, seeing no created thing in which some sparkle of God's glory could not be perceived, or in which his wisdom, goodness, beauty, and other perfections could not be observed. In the end they concluded that God is an eternal essence; the cause of every noble thing; true, good, just, and omnipotent; and that the first part of felicity therefore consists in contemplation of this most lofty, divine, and sovereign majesty. Then descending lower, and knowing that the sanctity and purity of God is such that it cannot receive anything that is not pure and holy, they introduced a number of works, virtues, and ways of living in agreement with human reason by which they measured God's will and the service that might please him. When they had thus introduced all of reason's works, virtues, and ways of living and placed them under the power of human strength, they used them to establish not only the rule and conduct for living well but also the virtue and efficacy of their sanctity and righteousness before God. This is how they added to the first point of felicity—which is the knowledge of God—the work and action proceeding from it, so that both points came to be comprehended under the term "virtue," which is man's final end.

When the of virtue is understood in this way to extend beyond that of moral virtue (as I have said), it indeed has some affinity with that point of virtue in which true and perfect human felicity consists, provided that it is better understood. For although the human mind speaks truthfully when, on the basis of certain demonstrations, it says that there is a God, it nevertheless errs when it tries to use human reason to understand the lofty and divine majesty itself and to know the nature of that majesty, which is infinite and incomprehensible to the human mind. The human mind then also errs when it tries to appease and gratify the divine majesty by its works when it cannot know God's will except as that of an angry judge. Christian doctrine, on the other hand, does not present God in his majesty, nor does it enjoin one to seek the divine nature so closely, fearing that the human mind will be dazzled by the splendor of his glory when it searches out that majesty too inquisitively. Rather, Christian doctrine posits God's will first of all as it is exhibited to us in Jesus Christ, who came in the flesh to fulfill our righteousness in it, and by his merit to present us as righteous, innocent, and cleansed of all filth. This is no barren, cold, and sterile knowledge devoid of fruit, as is the knowledge of human wisdom. It is most productive and fertile, abounding in fruits of love, confidence, hope, patience, invocation, thanksgiving, confession, praise for and glorification of his name, upright outward relations, and the performance of other good works that are inseparable from it and are done not out of any confidence in one's own righteousness as if we are justified by them and pleasing in God's eyes, since we know this virtue to belong to God alone. Rather, we do such works to testify of the love and honor we have for God, as well as of the obedience of sonship rather than slavery,[23] which we show to him as children who have been adopted by him and assured by his grace.

Even apart from its complete ignorance of God's will, philosophy also knows nothing of the power of sin, its dominion and tyranny over all people, and its cause, nor does it know that sin cannot be conquered by any created power. For if it did have this knowledge, it would not have erred in such futility and been so fixed on the desire to justify itself and make itself innocent—that is, by its wisdom and inventiveness as founded on human reason, and by its own works. Since all who followed philosophy rested on such a weak foundation, they remained in their faithlessness, doubt, despair, and ignorance, or even blasphemy against God, misusing his name. For to seek to be righteous before him on your own is to usurp his power, ravish his glory, and reject his grace. Thus, just as Pythagoras said that the good consists in unity and evil in multiplicity (that is, in all the ways one can go beyond and vary what is good simply in only one way),[24] so one must say that human righteousness and salvation consists in this one point of Jesus Christ alone, while every confidence and guide that goes beyond it is a lie and wicked and perverse. When virtue is understood in this way, it will doubtless be the sovereign good and true felicity—that is, what this knowledge of God resides in, communicating itself to us in his Son, and producing in us works to his

---

[23] Cf. Gal. 4:7; 1 Pet. 1:14.

[24] Cf. Aristotle, *Metaphysics* 1.5 (986a15–b2).

glory, and it is incomparably more excellent than moral felicity and anything else that philosophy may propose.

12. The tranquility and contentment of the mind are not true felicity.

And should someone say that aside from the end of this felicity there is yet another more distant and remote end to which the title of felicity more properly belongs (i.e., the tranquility and contentment of the mind, with eternal joy and bliss being proposed to man as his final good and felicity), we respond that it is not unfitting for an end to be the remotest and final chronologically, and yet not the principal end. Think, for example, of someone who abstains from evil first to conform to God's will, and then to protect his good name among his fellow men. He has two ends, and yet the final one in chronological terms is the less principal end. And when we speak of a final end, we understand that for which the others are principally made, and not the final chronological end which is concurrent with the others, as joy and bliss are with virtue. Nor is it any use to say that two goods united and joined together are more desirable than a single one, that virtue accompanied by health, beauty, strength, possessions, and the like is more complete and desirable than it is on its own, and so that virtue, not being desirable for its own sake alone (as we maintained for the sovereign good), cannot be felicity since it is altogether complete and self-sufficient. For the union and concurrence of several goods does not prevent that good where the point of felicity resides from always being preferable to all others, as the principal good among them. Thus, to say that two goods united together are more desirable than a single one must be understood according to its order and degree, so that the greater and better good is not lost for the lesser one—just as, if we could not keep virtue, goods, and riches simultaneously, it would be best to retain virtue and to lose the others. While we recognize that all things God created are good, we do so each according to its order, leaving us far from the Stoic view on this point.

13. Felicity is located in the soul, and not in bodily and external goods, and how the sovereign good of the Christian surpasses them all.

The philosophers who are thought to have spoken most accurately about man's sovereign good agree that it must be located in his most noble part, which sets him apart from all other creatures, and that it must be included among the good things that people can possess and that can more truly be deemed goods. We too locate man's sovereign good in the soul as man's most excellent part, which comes closest to God. However, we maintain that it cannot be included among the goods of fortune, as possessions and riches are called, nor the bodily goods, which are health, beauty, strength, nimbleness, and the like, nor even moral virtue insofar as our sovereign good cannot be found in us, but must be sought beyond ourselves in God. From this it follows that our sovereign good does not consist in acts of this virtue, even though we do confess that the work and act that is most proper to human beings is their true end. But humanity's true end does not consist in acts of virtue, since the end of virtue is only civil, political, and human tranquility. Rather, humanity's true end consists in acts of Christian virtue, whose end is God's glory. For even the Stoics say that just as all things are created to serve man, so too man is created to serve God.

Consequently, we easily see that our sovereign good, as Christian doctrine teaches us, far surpasses all the human opinions we treated above, and how it makes us much happier than whatever the philosophers have contrived. For those who thought that felicity is just living well said nothing that we do not say better. And this being the case, in what does living well consist, if not in the virtue we are discussing? As for those who wanted to locate it in either wisdom or prudence, they cannot equal us, given that true wisdom and prudence are comprehended under the virtue in which we constitute felicity, and the same is true even for all the moral virtues, albeit understood very differently from the way philosophy teaches them. And as for those who wanted to locate the sovereign good in joy, delight, and contentment of the mind, which they call pleasure, applying this name equally to both good and evil things—what pleasure could one find or imagine that is more enjoyable and lasting than the moral pleasure received in our felicity? Nor is this the end for which we say felicity must be loved, for to do so would rather be to love ourselves and therefore to make ourselves the final end and felicity: but it must be loved for the love of felicity itself, which (as we have said) is nothing other than God's glory. From this it follows that God's glory must be preferred not only over all goods, riches, honors, pleasures, and other advantages of life, but also over all political and human tranquility and felicity, and that no man ought to abandon it from any fear of evil, danger, poverty, exile, torment, and even death itself. Since whatever serves this end is not to be considered evil, dangerous, or fearful, so too nothing that does not fully relate to it ought to be considered good, useful, and profitable, such that the great difference between our felicity and that proposed by moral philosophy is easily perceived.

14. *The cause of felicity according to Aristotle, and according to the truth of Christian doctrine.*

When, as noted above, Aristotle says that moral felicity (even if it consists in the good of the soul as well as its operation) nevertheless needs corporeal and other external goods, since people cannot be happy if they lack health, strength, nimbleness, possessions, riches, and friends by which they can (as through instruments and tools proper to this end) do great and virtuous things, and since they cannot enjoy felicity when they do not have them, so he concludes, just as perfect virtue is necessary for felicity, so too is a full and complete life.[25] Aristotle furthermore adds that according to Solon no one can be said to be happy until the final day of his life because of the many changes and mutations to which the human condition is subject.[26] We, however, say that true felicity remains unscathed by any deficiency in bodily and external goods and that it does not reside in them, even though we do recognize these goods to be gifts of God, and that by knowledge of him, which is related by effect to his glory, we do experience some

---

[25] Aristotle, *Nicomachean Ethics* 1.9 (1100a4–5).
[26] Aristotle, *Nicomachean Ethics* 1.10 (1100a10–14).

felicity in this life, however miserable and brief it may be, until we enjoy it fully thereafter, provided that we persevere to the final point of life.

These, then, are the different views that exist on humanity's sovereign good and felicity. We wanted to give a brief overview of them to better understand which of them is most true, since by its nature truth is such that all true things in its proximity suddenly present themselves as one and of one accord with it, no more or less than the false things immediately appear to be dissimilar and altogether different from it.

But we now return to the virtue in which moral philosophy locates felicity and of which we have been speaking. We saw that there is a final end to human acts in which the sovereign good resides, and then what this sovereign good is like, and finally what moral felicity is. What now remains for us is to know its cause, that is, the means by which it can be acquired and from which it proceeds. When Aristotle poses this question, he responds waveringly, saying in the end that it is not certain whether moral felicity is received by good discipline, by the custom and exercise of good works, by fortune, or rather by divine will—and yet he adds that if God is the author and cause of the several good things we have, there is reason to think that he is the author and cause of that felicity which surpasses all other good things a person can receive. And even if, he continues, it was not from the immortal gods that moral felicity was sent to us, it at the very least ought still to be considered a divine thing.[27]

Yet in the end he states by way of conclusion that it is better to say that this felicity comes from us, and not from God or fortune, since it truly is acquired by human virtue through teaching, as well as through the habit and exercise of doing good, which are all means that are within the grasp of human power. He adds that every end is by nature universal and common to all since its natural virtue and power are not weakened, and consequently that felicity proceeds from human strength (for, so Aristotle says, if it came from God rather than nature, it would follow that this end is not common to us all), and that it is nothing but an operation of virtue, which is an effect proceeding from human causality. This is how Aristotle finally

---

[27] Aristotle, *Nicomachean Ethics* 1.9 (1099b9–17).

resolves the matter, so that we can see how ignorant philosophy really is of God's will toward us, not deeming it worthy to count on God's will with certainty for anything. For we do not want to deny reason's natural power for whatever pertains to the present life in any way, since reason has its precepts for civil and external morals, just like the other acts and sciences have their own, by means of which one can do things depending on reason, as we will show at greater length below. Nevertheless, it does not follow that we have to invent sources of this felicity and openly deny that it comes from God.

Therefore, the first thing we will say about the true felicity that we spoke of above, which resides in knowledge of God and in the faith in him we have through Jesus Christ, is this: it is a gift and light of God produced in us by his Holy Spirit, far removed from and beyond the knowledge and strength of human reason, so that we cannot acquire it by ourselves in any way. And as for moral felicity, if we follow Aristotle by including in it the goods, riches, health, a full and accomplished and long human life, together with the operations by virtue, we cannot say that all of this is within the power of man. But if we include only the acts and operations performed by virtue, we shall say that God has given us the sense and reason needed to aspire somewhat to this external and carnal righteousness, which is nevertheless altogether different from or even contrary to true and spiritual righteousness, as will be shown more clearly by what we will deduce at greater length below. But first we led our readers to understand what belongs to an understanding of moral virtue, and in what it consists.

Book Two

Book Two

1. Democritus's view of good and bad images in the air.

The philosopher Democritus said that we ought to pray for happy images to be presented to us in the air, and for good images proper and suitable to our nature to come to us rather than bad ones.[1] The other philosophers chided him for this, saying that he presupposed a false view and teaching in philosophy, leading people to vain superstition. I, however, think that if Democritus is properly understood, what he said was not so much to induce the human mind to think that there are apparitions in the air, as to induce people to pray to God to inspire them with good things and to propose to their thoughts certain images and impressions of virtue by which they might be incited to do what is good. And if this is so, what is better to seek or to ask for more urgently, what ought one to take greater pleasure in, and what is loftier or more difficult, than to be willing to correct and emend the vices of your morals, and to fashion your life and acts after the portrait of virtue's perfect image?

---

[1] See Plutarch, *De defectu oraculorum* 17.1 (*Moralia* 419a). Democritus (b. 460–457 BC) was one of the most important pre-Socratic philosophers, but only fragments of his works have survived.

The Right Use of Moral Philosophy

2. The science of morality must consider human nature, and Plato's view of it.

Having in the first book proposed and described this virtue in all its perfection as the virtue to which all our actions ought to be directed, we now must proceed (following Aristotle's order) to treat the moral and civil virtue necessary for the maintenance of human life and society. To this end we must first give some consideration to human nature, just as a physician must first pay attention to the natural inclination and disposition of the human body. In fact, for us this is even more necessary than it is for a doctor, since the science of morality (which is what we are treating here) is more excellent and better than medicine insofar as it treats of the soul, while medicine considers only the health of the body. This does not mean, however, that we need to provide a deep and subtle analysis of the soul and its parts, since that would involve greater difficulties than we have set before us. Rather, we will only go as far as the knowledge of this science requires.

3. The partition and division of the soul according to Plato and Aristotle.

When Plato speaks of the nature of man, he compares it to a sea monster called Scylla. Its upper part, he says, resembles a virgin, the middle a lion, and the bottom a barking dog.[2] Some think that he wanted to say that there are three souls in a person, or that the soul has three functions and duties. (For whether the soul is something distinct that is divided over several parts of the body, or rather a single thing that is in itself indivisible, just as circumference, convexity, and concavity are in a single round and hollow thing—this is a question without import for our present discussion.) And so, when Plato wanted to say that there are three souls, he located the lowest one in the liver, indicating that it resembles a dog, ready and inclined for every pleasure, and understanding it to be the natural virtue and force by which a person has nourishment, growth, and can also procreate. The middle part,

---

[2] Plato, *Republic* 9.588b–590a.

which he compared to a lion, he located in the heart, and it is where the passions and affections reside, such as anger and wrath, joy and sadness, hope and fear, hate, pity, and the like. The third and highest part he located in the head, and it is where the intellect, reason, memory, judgment, and the guide for voluntary movements are to be found. Plato was right to compare it to a virgin, being a person's completest and purest part.

Aristotle, however, divides the human soul into only two parts, the one rational and the other irrational, identifying as irrational that part where we located the virtue of nourishment and growth, which is common to herbs, plants, and all other things that sprout and take nourishment.[3] Here, however, we will say nothing more about this virtue since people do not accomplish any virtuous acts by it, for its primary activity takes place during sleep, when the wicked do not differ from the good. It was with this in mind that the ancients used to say that for half their lifetime the happy are no different from the miserable, except perhaps that the good by their better imaginations and thoughts sleep more softly and better than the rest. Apart from the virtue of nourishment and growth of which we have just spoken, the irrational part of the soul consists in yet another part that is indeed not rational of itself, but still participates in reason to some degree and is capable of it. This is the sensitive part of the soul, innately opposed to reason, although it still is such that it can be led by and ordered according to reason, as we see by experience in the difference between one person who abstains from pleasure and the other who cannot, since the former has reason as his master and the latter pleasure. However, it would be best to say that this sensitive part has some reason in it, like a son who obeys his father's reason, or a friend the admonition of another friend, and yet to maintain that this second part of the soul is twofold: one, such as the human mind, is where reason and judgment reside; the other, such as the sensitive part of man, does not have reason within and yet participates in it.

---

[3] Aristotle, *Nicomachean Ethics* 1.13 (1102a26–1103a10).

THE RIGHT USE OF MORAL PHILOSOPHY

4. The partition and division of virtues according to Plato and Aristotle, and that neither Plato nor Aristotle had knowledge of the principal intellectual virtues.

This, then, is a brief overview of the inner division of man, which one must know to better understand the division between the virtues as well. The one group of virtues, among them wisdom and prudence, is located in the understanding and the inner part where we have said reason resides. The virtues of the other group, such as generosity, temperance, and others that are properly speaking moral, are rather found in the sensitive part and in external acts, given that they are acquired by good morals and customs. For this reason, those who seek to praise someone for his morals and external works do not say that he is wise, sharp, prudent, and judicious, since that belongs to the intellectual virtues, but rather that he is gracious, generous, and moderate. So too those who want to praise someone for his intelligence, knowledge, and reason do not say that he is temperate or constant, but wise and prudent. This clearly shows the difference between the moral and intellectual virtues.

The Platonists divide the virtues in another way.[4] First there are the virtues they call "exemplary," which like the Ideas reside in a perfect, certain, and immutable understanding and knowledge of heavenly and human things, having even their perfect representations and figures enclosed in the mind. Then there are the virtues they call "purging," which purge the mind of every vice. And, finally, there are the "civil" virtues, which pertain to human civil life and society. We leave this division aside, however, and follow Aristotle's as the one that seems most suitable and fitting to us, and because the invention of such purging virtues hardly seems Christian to us since it attributes to human strength what people cannot at all have. We thus follow Aristotle in saying that virtue is to be understood and divided into two kinds, the one called "intellectual" and the other, "moral."[5] Intellectual virtue is so called because it resides in the action of the mind and because it for

---

[4] See Plotinus, *Ennead* 1.2; Porphyry, *Sententiae intelligibilia ducentes* 32.
[5] Aristotle, *Nicomachean Ethics* 2.1 (1103a15–19).

the most part is produced by and grows through the arts, sciences, and disciplines, and needs a lot of time and experience. Aristotle defers discussion of them until he has first treated moral virtue, maintaining his usual order of proceeding from the things that are closer, more familiar, and better known to those that are more distant, concealed, and hidden from us. Although he claims to treat these virtues elsewhere, he does not actually mention them anywhere else—I mean here the principal intellectual virtues that pertain directly to heaven and whose acts fully relate to God. For although some knowledge of God grows in us from the law of God, and although reason sees some evidence of him in nature, nevertheless there has been considerable confusion among the philosophers over the knowledge of God and of his providence, as must indeed happen whenever the human mind is not ruled and governed by the light of the gospel. In fact, philosophy does not have even a simple knowledge of the outward works of the law, and furthermore is completely ignorant of God's promises and their fulfilment, so that it has nothing to say about faith and the confidence it offers, about the hope in its aid, or about prayer and the other Christian intellectual virtues. For the teaching about these virtues has been revealed by the word of God, and even in a most certain manner by the voice of the gospel. When philosophy speaks about religion, it intends to speak only of a kind of reverence that human reason can imagine—that is, a reverence toward God the creator of heaven and earth, eternal and omnipotent, good, righteous, wise, to whom obedience is therefore due in the form of ceremonies and other things of human invention that philosophy considered sufficient to appease God's wrath toward sin. For that reason, we would seem to do well to speak at some length (and as succinctly as we can) about the Christian intellectual virtues as being first in order and the most important ones to know, especially since the perfection of the other virtues depends on them, as we will show more clearly in what follows when we uncover philosophy's ignorance in this regard, as well as the error that entered Christian doctrine when it extended moral philosophy too far.

5. The principal, Christian intellectual virtues.

These intellectual virtues are such that they teach us not only how we ought to be, but also how God is,[6] to the degree that we can understand it and as far as is necessary for us. It is also primarily by them that we are advised that we have been created after the image and likeness of God, and where and how we are to represent him here. The first intellectual virtue consists in knowledge of God by his Son, according to his promises and the gospel, together with a knowledge of man as a slave and serf to sin by the law, who produces only bad fruit and is therefore guilty to the point of death and eternal condemnation and in need of grace. The other is faith, which is nothing but a firm confidence and assurance of God's reconciliation with us through Jesus Christ, apart from which whatever anyone does is nothing but sin and displeasing to God. From this faith are born and produced almost all the other intellectual virtues: love for God, arising from this knowledge and persuasion of his goodness toward us; patience, which bears and endures the calamities we face on our own or together with others; prayer, with assurance of being heard at all times, whether in prosperity or during adversity; also thanksgiving, and the confession and proclamation of his name, with our mouth as well as our works and deeds, each according to his calling, turning away from all idolatry and false teaching and joining the true and pure church and gathering of believers. These are, in short, the principal intellectual virtues, which we will not treat at greater length here, since this is not the proper place because our main design was, after all, to treat only the moral virtues.

---

[6] La Place here refers to the attributes of God (*qualis sit Deus*), not his essence or being (*quid sit Deus*).

Book Two

6. The moral virtues, and, in the first place, how they are acquired, namely, whether it is by nature or by works.

To return to these moral virtues, the first thing we must do is to know how we acquire them and how they are produced in us, that is, whether this happens naturally and by nature, or rather by works. Following Pythagoras on this point, Socrates and Plato said that the soul was created by God with all its virtues, and that, since it forgets them when it enters the human body, it recalls them by learning.[7] Accordingly, there is no acquisition of new virtues in the proper sense, but rather a recollection of what had been forgotten. The Stoics claimed that virtues are produced in us by nature, so that nature is to be followed and retained as guide, and thus they made one's sovereign good the agreement of life with, and conformity to, nature. But if this were true, it would necessarily follow that the virtues are found equally in all people, since what comes from nature is common to all and immutable in all to the point of never changing by any contrary power or custom. We see this in each and every thing's natural inclination, such as a stone, whose natural inclination is always to fall and not rise, even if it were thrown up in the air thousands of times to try to accustom it to rising. In just the same way, the natural inclination of fire, which is to rise, cannot change and be accustomed to falling. Nor, similarly, can any other thing ever change to do what is against its natural inclination. It is therefore certain for all things that happen in us naturally, such as sight, smell, taste, hearing, and the like, that we first receive the natural forces and powers by which we see, smell, hear, and taste, as everyone can easily perceive in themselves.

Nor is there anyone who has received sight or hearing because he often saw and heard. On the contrary, people use sight and hearing because they have them, and it is not by using sight and hearing that we make them our own. It thus follows that the virtues are not acquired by nature, but—as we already said above—by good morals and customs, as the very name of these virtues indicates (for this is why they are called "moral virtues"). From this it follows that just as one becomes a smith by forging, a mason by laying bricks, and a harpist by playing

---

[7] See Plato, *Meno*, esp. 85d and 99e–100b.

the harp, so one becomes just, temperate, generous, and virtuous in other ways by performing acts of justice, temperance, generosity, and other virtues. All the good governors of cities and republics understood this well, and they clearly teach us this since, in order to instruct their citizens well and to make them good and upright, they do not leave them to the sole guidance of nature, but rather direct them to good morals and virtues by good laws and by doing what is upright and virtuous, offering a reward and recompense to these who do what is good, and punishment to those who act wickedly.

In order to show even more clearly that it is by works and acts that moral virtues are acquired, and not by nature, we might consider how virtues, just like the arts, are corrupted by the same things by which they are acquired—that is, by their acts and exercise in general. For the arts, we see how it is by plucking the strings that good and bad harpists are made, and by building and constructing that good and bad builders are made, and so on. If this were not so, it would follow in all the arts that every person would be naturally ignorant or naturally perfect, and that we would have no need for any master in order to learn these arts. So too when it comes to virtues, we see that it is by contracting, trading, negotiating, and managing affairs that some become just and others unjust, and for grand undertakings some become timid and cowardly and others tough and assured, and so also when it comes to pleasures, some are seen to become temperate and the others intemperate, some gentle and affable and others testy and bad-tempered—and all these things happen for no other reason than that some behave in one way, and the others another way. This clearly demonstrates that all habits, whether good or bad, come about and are produced in people by habituation and custom, and that they come from nothing but differing operations (i.e., good or bad) from which the diversity of habits proceeds. We therefore see how important it is to accustom the youth to one or another way of acting, since it is by acts and not simply by nature that the divide among us between virtue and vice is created. And just as a vessel long retains the smell of the liquid that had first been put in it, which is difficult to remove thereafter, so it is most difficult to change a way of life and the first morals to which people were accustomed from their very youth.

7. The science of morality resides more in the exercise and performance of good works, and not in knowledge, and the treatment of moral virtues by philosophy, provided that it is properly understood, does not conflict with Christian doctrine.

From the preceding argument it follows that the science of morality does not reside in knowledge and understanding of virtue, but in its works and exercise. And just as with theatrical plays we most esteem not those who are most knowledgeable but those who do are the best performers, so in order to become virtuous and upright people, as we really should be, knowledge of virtue is nothing without its exercise in good works, just as a body is nothing without its action and movement. Therefore, in treating of moral philosophy our first and principal consideration shall be to treat of works and acts, and of the way to perform them well, since from what we have said it follows that these are the principal causes of habit, that is, of the divide among us into one kind or the other, namely, virtue or vice. Nor ought anyone to think that these moral and political virtues rightly understood, which serve to preserve human society, conflict with Christian doctrine (any more than political laws and ordinances do), provided that we do not place any foundation of inward righteousness there. For at this point we are dealing only with an external and human justice, rather than a divine justice. Even Christian doctrine recommends that one develop the custom of doing good works, so every person might be diligent in not giving free reign to his passions and pleasures. This requires and demands our singular diligence. It is completely inconsistent with all discipline to think that human effort and power serves no purpose here and is useless.

8. By what works virtue is acquired, and how virtue, once acquired, produces works that fully resemble those from which it was first produced.

Now that we have seen that virtue is not acquired by nature but by works, according to the rule and teaching of moral philosophy, we must now show which works they are. We can easily know this from the opposite, that is, by indicating the works by which virtue is lost, namely, those that consist in extreme and vice. For all things that are lost and corrupted by their extremes are acquired and preserved by their mean, as we easily see in what is outward and plain—for when we deal with things that are occult and hidden, we have to use evidence that is plain and manifest. We thus see, for example, how it is by excessive work on the one hand, and excessive laziness on the other (which are two extremes), that the human body loses its powers. So too excessive drinking and eating on the one hand, and excessive abstinence on the other, break down health. Therefore, moderate work and living, which are the means between two extremes, acquire and preserve the one and the other. We shall say the very same about the inward, as when someone becomes timid and cowardly by always being surprised and scared by all things without reason, but reckless and careless when he exposes himself excessively to every danger and takes every risk. And between these two extremes that corrupt virtue, holding to the mean is the way to acquire the virtue called "strength" or "constancy." Likewise people become intemperate by abandoning themselves completely to pleasure, but stupid and unfeeling by fleeing them altogether—which are the two extremes. So too, holding to the mean is the way to acquire the virtue called "temperance," and the same holds true for other virtues. It therefore becomes clear that the works that consist in the middle are those by which virtues, of which we will speak at greater length below, can be acquired.

One must also know that once these virtues have been acquired and produced by such works, they produce similar works, that is, works that—no more or less than the former works by which the virtues were acquired—also consist in the mean. And just as we see in the case of human strength, that it is acquired by work and labor, and that once it has been acquired, strength disposes a person well to labor, in the same way we become temperate by abstaining from pleasures. And once we have become temperate, we abstain from pleasures. In just the same way, we become strong and stouthearted by developing the custom of disregarding frightful things; and once we have become strong, we await frightful things without being taken aback by them. These, in sum, are the works by which a person acquires the habit of virtue, and they are the same works that that person does and produces once he has developed the habit of doing them.

9. The way to know when the habit of virtue will be formed in someone.

Nevertheless, in order to know when a person has developed the habit of virtue, it is not sufficient simply to consider the works that he produces (regardless of how close they are to the mean, and seem good and virtuous), nor even their frequency and great number. Rather, one must first look to see whether they are done with pleasure, since pleasure and displeasure are the principal marks and clearest signs by which we know whether or not the habit has been formed, and they better reveal the habit and show its true nature. When a person appears displeased and bored when doing what is good, this is a clear sign that the habit of virtue is not present there. But if such works are done with pleasure, this is clear proof that the habit of virtue has been fully fashioned there. For example, if someone derives pleasure from abstaining from his desires, this is a certain sign of the habit of temperance. But if, on the contrary, that person shows regret and displeasure, it is a sign of the opposite habit of intemperance. And someone who cheerfully (or at least patiently) bears adversities shows the habit of strength and constancy in him, whereas someone who impatiently endures these adversities reveals the opposite. From this it is clear that each habit formed in us has exactly the same power as our natural forces of sight, hearing, taste, smell, and touch, which enable us to see, hear, taste, smell, and touch without difficulty and with pleasure. For also the habit to either virtue or vice, once it has been fashioned in us, performs its operations as if it does so of itself, with pleasure and without any difficulty.

10. Habit is primarily concerned with pleasure and displeasure, and humanity's true institution concerns these two points.

Now just as we said that pleasure and displeasure are the principal marks for discerning whether a person has the habit of virtue, so too we ought to know that the entire question and difficulty concerning virtue is found in making good use of this pleasure and pain. All things that by their good use are causes for acquiring the habit of virtue are by their evil use the cause of the destruction of the habit of virtue and the creation of its opposite. We see this in the pleasure for which we perform a thousand wicked acts, and in the pain for fear of which we neglect the performance of an infinite number of good and virtuous things. For this reason Plato, knowing that the principal difficulty of human life is found at the point of pleasure and pain, very wisely said that the true nourishment and institution of man is to accustom him from infancy to rejoice or grieve over the things one ought rightly to rejoice or grieve over.[8] For it is certain that no human act or affection fails to be accompanied by either pleasure or pain, teaching us that the main difficulty for developing the habit of virtue concerns these two points. For rewards and recompenses (which are pleasant) are proposed to the good, and punishments and chastisements (which are painful) to the evil, for no other end than to entice people to take pleasure in doing good and displeasure in doing evil. Punishments serve to keep the soul in virtue, just as medicines serve to keep the body in health, since it is by their contraries that illnesses are healed. And since the habit to virtue works primarily at these two points of pleasure and pain, there is no doubt that it naturally depends on the things that make it better or worse, among which we first of all include pleasures and delights, and pains and displeasures—that is to say, so as to pursue or flee them in an unfitting manner.[9]

---

[8] Plato, *Republic* 5.462b–c.

[9] "in an unfitting manner": The meaning of the French *autrement qu'il n'appartient* here is unclear.

11. We must not locate the end of pleasure and displeasure in ourselves.

We must, however, see to it that we do not locate the end of this pleasure and pain in ourselves in any way, nor in moral philosophy, whose end is public uprightness and utility, as well as all other things pertaining to the good of human society. For both pleasure and pain must necessarily be related to a more distant end, which is respect for God's honor, so that when we do good and virtuous works, we take pleasure in obeying and honoring him. When we on the contrary do wrong, the displeasure we feel must not be as that of Alexander when he had killed his good friend Cleitus, prompting Anaxarchus to say: "Here is Alexander, weeping like a slave, in fear of the law and the censure of men."[10] Rather, our pain must be for the disobedience and dishonor we showed toward God, since the end of virtue is his glory alone, as we have said above.

12. The task of virtue, and the false view of the Stoics in this regard.

Thus the task of virtue properly speaking is to temper and settle what pleasure and pain trouble and stir up. This is why the Stoics said that virtue is nothing but a certain tranquility and rest, void of all affections and passions. But since we cannot deny that there are in us affections that agree with reason or even serve as principal foundations of virtues, this definition, which completely strips man of all the affections with which he was born, was found to be much too harsh. For the attempt to deprive people of all affections seeks to remove nature altogether, which has given us affections as instruments and goads necessary for exercising our actions. Accordingly, it would have been better for them to say that virtue is a moderation of a person's natural appetites and impulses, and not simply the privation of all affections. Although great men have sought to sustain this view by claiming that it agrees with the gospel, albeit with the qualification that privation of all affections

---

[10] Plutarch, *Lives. Alexander* 52.3. English translation from Bernadotte Perrin, trans., *Plutarch's Lives*, vol. 7 (Cambridge, MA: Harvard University Press, 1919), 375.

belongs only to the most perfect life renewed by the Holy Spirit, they deceived themselves in this. For the Holy Spirit does not deprive us of all our affections but rather gives us good affections, and corrects and refashions those that are bad. There is, after all, a great difference between the Christian and moral virtues, insofar as the former are affections placed in us by the Holy Spirit, while the latter are not affections at all but particular habits regulating and tempering people's external works, as we have just explained.

13. The proper nature of virtue concerns pleasure and displeasure, and the main difficulty is discerning and choosing well between the two.

But to return to our main discourse, it is sufficiently clear from what we have written that virtue's true natural inclination is to produce good things with pleasure and pain, just as it is natural for vice, on the contrary, to do what is bad with pleasure and pain. For the rest it is certain that there are three things, as Aristotle says, that we naturally long for and pursue—that is, what is upright, profitable, and delightful—just as there are three things we naturally hate and shun—namely, what is corrupt, hurtful, and boring.[11] As people find themselves surrounded by all these things and are drawn toward different views and volitions, the virtuous perform good works, while those who are led by vice do what is evil, being primarily pulled and drawn by delight and pleasure, which we share with all animals and which are nourished and grow along with us from our very infancy and childhood, so that it is most difficult to separate ourselves from it.

Moreover, we all form a natural judgment on our works and acts by the pleasure and pain that follow from them, although this varies from person to person. The main task of virtue is, therefore, to discern and choose well between the one and the other, since it is of utmost importance to human action to delight in or abhor well or poorly something, and to enjoy or lament it well or poorly. For pleasure is an alluring mistress, by which we are gladly deceived and enslaved. Although I consider nothing more true than what Heraclitus said—

---

[11] Aristotle, *Nicomachean Ethics* 2.3 (1104b30–1105a1).

namely, that it is much more difficult to resist pleasure than anger and wrath[12]—the force of wrath, however strong and vehement it may be, is nevertheless altogether different from that of pleasure, which is our close, intimate, and customary friend. Plato thus says that pleasure is everyone's principal bait and strongest lure toward evil.[13] But also virtue's excellence, just as that of art, is to lead to great, arduous, and difficult things. This is why we already said on several occasions that virtue above all concerns pleasure and displeasure, delight and pain.

14. Whether one becomes good by doing good works, or whether one must first be good to do what is good.

Since, as we have sufficiently shown, virtue according to the philosophers is not in us by nature but is acquired by works in the manner we indicated, it follows that one becomes good by doing good works, and evil by doing what is evil. So one becomes just by doing what is just, and unjust by doing unjust works; one becomes temperate by doing what is temperate, and intemperate by doing intemperate things; and so on. Several philosophers have, however, resisted this conclusion, and claimed instead that one must first be good in order to do what is good, just to do what is just, and temperate to do what is temperate. According to them, people who do what is good, just, and temperate are already good, just, and temperate, just as we call someone who does what pertains to the art of painting a painter, and someone who does what belongs to the art of music a musician. And the same holds for other arts and sciences, which people must have before they can exercise them. But to restrict ourselves to the terms and limits of philosophy, by whose terms we are after all speaking, this view cannot stand. For the example and arguments from the arts do not hold in this regard, since it is possible for someone to do something artistic without having knowledge of it, either randomly, or else with someone else's guidance, or in some other way. Accordingly, in order to say that something has been done according to the art of painting or music, it

---

[12] See Aristotle, *Nicomachean Ethics* 2.3 (1105a8).

[13] Plato, *Timaeus* 69c3–d6.

suffices for that thing to have been done according to the teaching of the art of painting or music, even though the one who does it may have no knowledge of it whatsoever. But even if we assume for the sake of argument that no one can make a work of art unless he has knowledge of it, there is nevertheless a great difference between virtue and the arts, so that the comparison between them does not hold true. For in order to say that something was done according to art, it suffices for that thing to have been done according to what art requires, since things done by art have their perfection in themselves. But in order to say that a work is just, temperate, or otherwise virtuous, it is not enough to consider that work in itself, regardless of how virtuous it may appear to be. Rather, one must also consider the way the one who did it operates, that is, how that person behaved in doing it—whether he did it knowledgeably and with good affection, by good judgment and reason, with a firm determination and an unchanging will. For if it were done randomly, flippantly, by some force and vehemence of nature, without deliberation, by hypocrisy and dissimulation, for some specific purpose (like Alcibiades, when he completely adapted himself to the Spartans while in their city[14]), or some other unfitting way—in all such cases we cannot say that the deed was done virtuously. Therefore, when we say that it is by doing virtuous things that one becomes virtuous, we mean to speak of works done by right judgment and will, and it is by the custom of doing them—and with pleasure, as we have said—that one acquires the habit of virtue. From this it follows that one becomes virtuous by doing works of virtue, and that human works and acts merit the name of virtue when they are such that a virtuous person who has acquired the habit of virtue would do them. For, as we have said above, the works we do after we acquire the habit of virtue are entirely similar to those from which the habit of virtue was produced.

---

[14] Plutarch, *Lives. Alcibiades* 15.1.

15. People usually derive greater pleasure from knowing good things than from doing them.

From the above it follows that works of the arts and sciences differ considerably from those of virtue, since knowledge of the specific art in question is the very least of the things required. People are generally dissatisfied with this, however, and consider that it is sufficient to read, understand, and know what pertains to virtue, and to be able to talk and discourse about it, without giving any thought to the performance of what is good. But this is no different from sick people being altogether ready for and diligent in hearing and listening to the advice of their physician, and glad to talk and dispute about it, but otherwise unwilling to do anything the doctor prescribes. For just as one cannot be healed by talking of medicinal remedies, so one must not expect to become a good and virtuous person simply by delighting in the knowledge, understanding, and discussion of virtue. Epictetus spoke wisely in this respect when he said that sheep do not vomit the grass they have eaten to show the shepherds how much they took in, but rather digest it within so as to show their beautiful wool on the outside.[15] So too we ought not to devote any effort to trying to show the virtue we have learned by talking and chatting about it, but we ought rather to digest it well and show some of its effects by our works. To that end, we highly recommend everyone consider what was said of Aristides:

> He wishes not to seem just, but rather to be just,
> And reap a harvest from deep furrows in a mind
> From which there spring up honorable counselings.[16]

---

[15] Epictetus, *Enchiridion* 46.

[16] Plutarch, *Lives. Aristides* 3.4. English translation adapted from Bernadotte Perrin, trans., *Plutarch's Lives*, vol. 2 (Cambridge, MA: Harvard University Press, 1914), 221.

16. The will, and a person's inner parts that precede it.

But since for virtue the main thing to be considered is the work, and since the work is judged primarily by the will because it is what produces the work (I still speak here according to the precepts of moral philosophy, waiting to speak of Christian doctrine later), it follows that we must say something of the will so that we may better know how it ought to be in order to meet the requirements of virtue. One thing we have to know is that whatever can be proposed to us—that is, to our eyes, or to our imagination and thinking—is such that it can appear as either good or evil, and that in different ways (by pleasure or pain) it causes a sudden emotion in us. This emotion we call an "affection," an internal part in us that is the first to receive the impression of the object, and it is touched and taken hold of by the thing proposing itself, to the point of wanting to pursue it immediately or else to flee and abandon it. But before one or the other can happen, there is another part in us, namely reason, whose seat Aristotle locates in the heart,[17] and it consults and deliberates whether what has entered the affection is good or evil, and profitable or hurtful, and so whether the thing ought to be followed or abandoned. And after this deliberation comes choice, which chooses what it finds to be good according to the report of reason, and then, to finish the matter (internally, I mean), the will follows, producing works externally. It is by the custom of doing these works by this right will that the habit of virtue, of which we have been speaking, is generated.

17. Deliberation.

Therefore, the first deliberation is of the things that have entered the affection—not all, but only those about which a person with sense and reason would ponder as being in our power, albeit uncertain and doubtful, and liable to go in one direction or the other. Now people ponder not only whether the thing that has entered affection ought to be pursued or done, but also the means serving to lead and guide

---

[17] Cf. Aristotle, *On the Motion of Animals* 703a13ff.

them toward it, and, if multiple means are available, which one of them is the best, and, if there is only one, how one might be aided by it. People therefore do not stop investigating until they have reached this first point for which they initially entered into deliberation, although in that deliberation this first point nevertheless proves to be the last.

18. Choice, and how it is not the same thing as will, pleasure,[18] or opinion.

Next comes choice, which uses reason to investigate and choose what it determines is the best action, and is a close friend of virtue. Choice gives a clearer demonstration of people's morals than their works themselves do, and although it is voluntary, it still is not the same thing as the will, since even children and all animals do have a will, but do not participate in choice. So too those who suggested that choice is the same thing as pleasure, or even opinion, are deceived. For pleasure is shared with brute beasts, whereas choice belongs only to human beings. Likewise, an intemperate person acts from pleasure, but not from choice, while conversely a temperate person acts by choice rather than pleasure. And, finally, pleasure often becomes so agitated by sudden emotions that one cannot say the act was a result of choice. As for opinion, it cannot be the same thing as choice. For an opinion concerns both true and false things, while choice pertains to what is good and evil, and no one is identical to his opinions, while everyone is the same as his choice. After all, to have the opinion that justice is preferable to injustice, it does not follow that the person who has this opinion is just, but it does follow that they are just who choose justice and abandon injustice. Furthermore, if opinion were the same thing as choice, it would suddenly follow that we have an opinion on something merely because we choose it. Yet this conflicts with the truth, for we form opinions much more often than we choose. Choice, therefore, is a voluntary selection of one out of two or more things investigated by reason.

---

[18] *cupidité*.

19. The will, what ought to be called voluntary or forced, and the difference between something done by ignorance and something done ignorantly.

Since the will is the next and final consideration, completing the inner work, the philosophers have held that it is a certain internal virtue and power by which we, under reason's suasion, approve, consent, and acquiesce to whatever has entered our affection and desire. Or, we reprove, resist, and reject it. For of itself the will has no light, except insofar as it receives light from judgment and reason, which has been given to it not as its mistress, but as a counsel, guide, and director, showing it what it ought to do, and is that which (as it were) deliberates over what the will produces. Nevertheless, the will retains such mastery and command over affection, deliberation, and choice that it does not place anything of what has entered affection into deliberation unless it pleases it, and, once it has placed it there, it is up to the will to withdraw or delay it, or to defer it to another time, or else to resolve not to do anything with it, just as for a prince his will is his reason. Yet to do this, the will still has some appearance of goodness inciting it to do that. For even if the will was thought to have great freedom (we will speak of it at greater length below), it is only with difficulty that it wills what is wicked, and it does so only when that wicked thing comes to it under the appearance of some good, commodity, or pleasure.

A thing is thus (according to this doctrine, and still without leaving the terms of philosophy) said to be voluntary—that is, done by pure will, either from virtue or vice—when its first beginning and motive issues from us. On the contrary, something is termed forced and constrained when its motive and cause proceeds from outside its executor, who makes no contribution of his own. We added this with a view to things that are indeed done by force and constraint, even though consent was given at the time of their execution. For such things are considered to be partly forced and partly voluntary, since they are indeed voluntary with respect to the time when they were done, so as to avoid greater misfortune. Likewise, things done by ignorance cannot be considered voluntary but are rather forced, provided that remorse follow the deed. For if no remorse follows, such things are more properly said to be involuntary, just as, properly speaking, we say that something done by a person who has lost control due to wine or anger was done not by ignorance (insofar as it appears that it was done by anger or drunkenness), but ignorantly since it was not done with knowledge. We also do not say that the wicked do evil by ignorance. For that would mean that what they did is pardonable. We do maintain that the wicked sin ignorantly, that is, without knowing how to distinguish well between good and evil, since their judgment is corrupt and depraved. This allows us to understand better and see more clearly what we stated above, namely, that works are judged as performed virtuously when done by right reason and will.

20. Comparison between human justification according to Christian doctrine and the justification taught by philosophy.

This, then, is how the civil, political, and human works of which moral philosophy speaks justify no one—that is, they do not make the person who does them morally and humanly good and just in the eyes of people—unless they are done with a right reason and a good will. For this philosophy does not have God as its object and final cause, but only the common utility of the republic. The philosophers call this common utility of the republic "right reason," and by it Aristides, Phocion, Cato, Fabius,[19] and others who did excellent things for their republic were justified, that is, held and reputed to be righteous. Such is the human justice of which moral philosophy speaks, according to which to do good works is only to do them by this right judgment and intention, regardless of how good, virtuous, and just these works might otherwise appear to be. But Christian righteousness is an altogether different thing, and differs as widely from human justice as heaven does

---

[19] Aristides (5th c. BC) was an Athenian politician. Phocion (402/1–318 BC) was a statesman and general in Athens and a pupil of Plato. Cato the Elder (ca. 234–149 BC) was an archconservative Roman and an important cultural, military, and political figure. Quintus Fabius Maximus Verrucosus (ca. 280–203 BC) was a Roman statesman and general who was elected dictator to resist Hannibal in the Second Punic War.

from earth. This is why those who wanted to apply moral philosophy to Christian righteousness erred gravely, mixing and confusing human and divine matters with great temerity and ignorance.

Christian righteousness does not depend on our works in any way, since it is a righteousness received from outside of ourselves, not by doing righteousness but only by grasping it in faith and believing that God made Jesus Christ to be our righteousness. This is truly a hidden and mysterious righteousness considered foolishness by human wisdom.[20] Moral philosophy, not leaving its boundaries, rightly judges the goodness of a work by the person's reason, intention, and will, without looking to the appearance of that goodness, and it says that a good and just person is not one who simply does good and just works, but does them by this right will. In a similar way, Christian doctrine judges the goodness of the work, looking to the heart, not as we have received it by nature with its corrupted and depraved affections because of sin, but as it has been cleansed and purified by faith. Therefore, just as it is the will and reason that properly justifies a person morally, so it is faith, purifying and cleansing reason and the will, that justifies a person Christianly, the former before men and the other before God, who does not look upon the human heart as blemished, nor to the person's intention if he has not already been cleansed, or rather, totally renewed, which can only happen by faith. And this is why it is written that God first had regard for Abel, rather than his offering,[21] which means only that Abel's offering and works pleased God because of his faith, without which no one can do anything pleasing to God, since whatever is done without faith is only sin.[22]

Everything done by human reason but without faith is displeasing and offensive to God. There is good reason for this. Faith attributes and gives all glory to God, believing him to be true in his promises, gracious, merciful, the author and dispenser of every good thing, and so faith is, as it were, the creator of his divinity in us. Reason, on the other hand, pulls all the glory toward itself, since it wants to justify

---

[20] 1 Cor. 1:18–31.
[21] Gen. 4:4.
[22] Rom. 14:23.

itself by itself and is persuaded that God is an angry judge who wants to be appeased by our works, chiding him for lying in all that he has promised and rejecting his grace together with all its benefits. Reason ought therefore to restrict itself and remain within its limits, which do not extend beyond whatever belongs to truth and moral justice, what Saint Paul called "righteousness of the flesh."[23] And as regards one's justification before God, reason must leave this to faith, so as to stay on earth without trying to ascend to the heavens. For faith is considered not as a work proper to the person, but as God's particular gift to him, by which he performs his works in an altogether different way than before. For just as philosophy says on its own terms that a person cannot be ready and prepared to do what is good and virtuous with pleasure and as is fitting without a certain habit produced in him by having become accustomed to doing well, likewise we say according to the terms of Christian doctrine that a person cannot do anything right if he does not have faith in, and certain persuasion of, God's goodness.

21. How human beings have always been inclined to attribute justice to their works, and how the error of the scholastics' view arose from philosophy.

Those who wanted to apply the justice of right reason and will to Christian righteousness[24] failed to consider its outward filth and plagues, such as unbelief, doubt, distrust, contempt, hatred, and rebellion against God, and looked only to the misguided righteousness of works, which are nothing but brooks streaming from these sources. This is why they easily attribute justice to this works righteousness, claiming that God accepts them, not because that is our due, but because it is fitting that it be so. For the good works done before grace, they say, cause grace to be imparted as is fitting, and the works done after the imparting of grace merit eternal life insofar as they are worthy of it. For God is in no way indebted when it comes to the former

---

[23] Cf. Rom. 8:4; Gal. 3:3.
[24] *justice*.

category of works. Rather, insofar as he is good and righteous, it is altogether reasonable for him to approve of them, or, when they are done in mortal sin, for him to give grace for such service. But after grace, God does become a debtor, and he is constrained by right to give eternal life; for that work is not just according to its substance a work originating from free will, but also one done in grace performing grace, that is, in dilection.

This, in short, is what it is to apply moral philosophy to theology. For suppose it were true what they claim, namely, that while in mortal sin we can do some small work that not only pleases God according to its substance, but also can merit grace congruently, as they say, and that after having received this grace we can do works according to grace (that is, according to dilection) and acquire the right to eternal life—if what they claim is true, then what need would we have for the grace of God, the remission of our sins, the promise, deliverance from death, and the victory of Christ, since we have our free choice and our natural forces, which are sufficient for doing a good work by which we merit grace congruently, and thereafter eternal life, by the merit of our work? In sum, all this is only to say what moral philosophy claims, namely, that by right reason and a good will we do good and just works, by which we acquire the habit of virtue, and that, once this habit of virtue is fashioned in us, it produces virtuous works that justify us morally.

Those who are so arrogant and ignorant as to mix what belongs to human righteousness with divine justice have much less reason for excuse than the philosophers who had no knowledge of God, since they limited and confined their doctrine to the civil, political, and human, while the former with great temerity and no less ignorance transported natural and human matters to heaven, and mixed and confused them with the divine. And if, as Scotus and Ockham say,[25]

---

[25] La Place presents John Duns Scotus (ca. 1266–1308) and William of Ockham (ca. 1288–1348) as respresentatives of a stream of medieval scholastic theology that taught that human beings could receive divine grace by doing naturally good acts that were within their power to do. See Richard A. Muller, *Dictionary of Latin and Greek Theological Terms*, 2nd ed. (Grand Rapids: Baker Academic, 2017), s.v. "facere quod in se est."

it is true that people by their natural powers can love creation, a young man a beautiful girl, and a greedy person money, which are lesser goods, why can they not also love God, who is a much greater good? If people by their natural powers have dilection for creation, they will much more, as they say, have dilection for the creator, as if someone who has the power of the lesser, has the power of the greater. Thereafter they add that we always have to do good until we know there to be no more sin in us, for the true way to justify ourselves is to do what is in us. And when we do what is in us, God infallibly gives grace. And they do not understand the power to do what is in oneself in too strict a sense, but think that it suffices for that power to be understood in a physical sense, not in a mathematically indivisible way, which cannot obtain—that is, it suffices for a person to do what can count on the approval of the judgment of an excellent man.[26] This, as I have said, is simply to follow moral philosophy, which says that a virtuous work is one that a virtuous person would do or approve. And so, they say, we ought not to doubt that grace will follow, not because of any merit performed prior to grace, but because God will not fail to do it, for he is so good and just that it is impossible for him not to do it for the good that is thought to have been done. This is to return always to the point of moral philosophy, namely, that people justify themselves by the good works done by their good will and right reason. According to this theory, it follows that those who govern their family, build a house, exercise the magistracy, or do any other political, domestic, or natural thing, doing what is in them, truly have an excuse. However, this cannot be adapted to spiritual, celestial, and divine matters, in which people can do nothing but sin, since they have been sold under sin.[27]

---

[26] Cf. John Duns Scotus, *God and Creatures: The Quodlibetal Questions*, trans. Felix Alluntis and Allan B. Wolter (repr., Washington, DC: The Catholic University of America Press, 1981), q. 17 (pp. 388–98). See Thomas M. Osborne Jr., *Human Action in Thomas Aquinas, John Duns Scotus & William of Ockham* (Washington, DC: The Catholic University of America Press, 2014), 185–220.

[27] Cf. Rom. 7:14.

These men do indeed confess human nature to be corrupt, but they say that people's natural quality remains intact and consequently that the mind is pure and the will good and whole, thereby concluding that it is possible for people to justify themselves by their works. We do not deny that one's natural quality, such as the will, remains to some degree with respect to natural matters. What we do deny is that it remains for spiritual matters, since, as we have said, the human mind as well as the will are corrupt and depraved, and even hostile to God. Therefore, when it comes to domestic, civil, and political matters, right reason and good will do indeed justify—that is, the works and those who perform them are by these works considered good and just in the eyes of others in whose presence they receive glory. But in ecclesiastical and spiritual matters, it is faith alone that justifies us, and it is by faith alone that we begin to do good and just works. For, as we will say below, just as virtue has two principal effects (i.e., perfectly disposing the person in which it is found, and rendering that person's work perfect and complete), so too faith, which is an infinite virtue, disposes the person in whom it is found in singular perfection, and also renders that person's work entirely perfect and complete, insofar as it grasps the entire and perfect righteousness of Christ and communicates it to us. We wanted to make this clear so as to show how great is the error of confusing this philosophy with Christian doctrine, and to demonstrate that philosophy must not be extended beyond its boundaries and limits. Now, however, it is time to consider what virtue is.

Book Three

Book Three

We have, therefore, seen how virtue is not in us naturally and is rather acquired by works—not all works, but those that consist in an intermediate point. Then we saw how we can know that virtue is acquired by and formed in us, and how, once fashioned there, it produces works that are altogether similar to those from which it was produced. We also saw that virtue resides between delight and pain, that is, between pleasure and displeasure. We furthermore demonstrated how it is by doing good and virtuous works that a person becomes good and virtuous, but that to identify a work as having been done virtuously, it is not enough just to consider the work in itself, nor the person's understanding of virtue, but that we must above all see whether it has been done by right reason and a good will. We also noted the difference between moral philosophy and Christian doctrine in this regard. And so, having considered all that we judge to belong to virtue and as necessary for knowing how moral virtue is acquired and in what it consists, we will now investigate virtue more closely, so that we may know what it is.

To this end, we need to recall that there are in the soul (the seat of virtue, as we have said) three things that are the principles and sources from which all our actions flow—namely, the affections, the powers, and the habits, and it is in one of these that we must locate virtue. These three things are in that part of the soul which, as we noted above, participates in reason without being fully rational; it is called the "appetitive" part inasmuch as the natural appetites for the things presenting themselves to us reside there. And since the diversity of the things that present themselves to us causes sudden emotions in us in equally different ways, by pleasure or pain, we call these emotions "affections" and "passions." Among them are concupiscence, anger, fear, confidence, envy, joy, friendship, hatred, jealousy, compassion, and pity, and, in a word, all other things of a similar nature that are accompanied by pleasure and pain. And inasmuch as there are parts in us that are proper for satisfying and fulfilling these affections (i.e., the parts by which we can love, hate, lament, be angry, and the like), we call them "powers." In respect to the habits, we have already shown that they are nothing but a certain form of virtue or vice that grows from one's morals by the exercise and custom of doing good and evil, and by which the works performed are good or evil. Accordingly, we say of someone who is too impetuous and furious in his anger, or too slow in or indifferent to it, that he has a poor habit of anger, while, on the contrary, we say of those whose disposition in their anger is at the intermediate point, that they have a good habit of anger. The same holds true for all the other human affections, as we will show at greater length and in detail below.

1. What virtue is, whether it is affection, power, or habit.

Now, however, it is time to consider whether virtue is an affection, power, or habit. As we said above, it must be one of these. First of all, virtue cannot be an affection, since people are generally not considered good or evil by their affections alone, while this does hold true for virtue and vice. Similarly, on the whole no one is praised or scolded simply for becoming angry or afraid, but for how they become so, while each and every person is certainly considered to merit either blame or praise for their virtues or vices. Moreover, we enter the affections of anger, fear, and the rest unawares, while virtues are produced from deliberate acts. And, finally, we are moved by the affections so as to be overcome by them, while by the virtues we are disposed to do what is good.

BOOK THREE

2. Virtue is habit, and what this habit is.

These same reasons lead us to conclude that the virtues also cannot be powers, since we cannot be praised or scolded for them (i.e., simply for being able to become angry or fearful), since no one is good or bad simply for having the power to do something. Moreover, virtue, as we have said above, is not in us by nature, while the powers are naturally in us. If, therefore, the virtues are neither affections nor powers, it must follow that they are habits. Nor does it help to posit what some have suggested, namely, that the mean between two extremes must be considered to be of the same kind as the extremes—that, since virtue is between two extremes of affection, it must be considered an affection rather than a habit, given that the mean and intermediate point indeed cannot be of another kind than its extremes. But we say that virtue is between two habits that are extremes and belong to vice, at a laudable intermediate point, and that it is therefore rightly said to be a habit, rather than a power or affection. With this we think we have sufficiently shown to what genus or kind virtue belongs.

Nevertheless, it is not enough just to know in general that a virtue is a habit, without understanding with greater precision what this habit is like, that is, its condition and character. To this end, we have to know that virtue of itself, regardless of where it is found, always has two main effects: the one is that it perfectly orders the thing in which it is found, and the other is that it also renders that thing's work perfect. This can be seen in the virtue of the eye, which makes the eye beautiful, clear, and perfect, and also renders its vision most perfect. Similarly, the virtue of a horse renders it good and courageous, as well as swift in running, ready to carry a rider, and stout in combat. The same applies uniformly in all other things in which virtue is found, especially people. Virtue first of all renders them good, and then it also renders their works and acts good. Now we have already shown above how and in what way that happens, but this will become even clearer when we proceed to consider the nature of virtue more closely.

3. The arithmetic method and the geometric method.

To this end we do well to recall that in all things that allow division, there can be too much, too little, and what is equal, relative to either the divisible thing or to us. We call "equal" what is between too much and too little (i.e., between what is excessive and what is deficient), but equidistant from the two extremes; this is called the "mean" relative to the thing divided in this way. For in all divisible things, the mean will always appear equal in all ways, as the center of the earth is in relation to its circumference. This can be seen most clearly in mathematics, as with the number six, for example, which is equally between the numbers two and ten, since there is no more between two and six than there is between six and ten, as the number six is equidistant from each extreme represented by the other numbers. When the mean is understood in this way, it is also called the "arithmetic mean," and to arrive at it one never considers anything but the equal distance from the two extremes.

But as for the other mean, which we have described as not relative to an object but to us, it is called "geometric," and there is a great difference between it and the arithmetic mean. For when we are dealing with it, we have no regard for the distance between extremes, but only for a certain reasonable and equal proportion relative to us rather than to the thing, according to the specific consideration of each person, which differs from all others and is not common to them. For example, if ten francs is too much for a person's upkeep and two francs too little, it does not follow that six francs (according to the arithmetic mean) is average and reasonable. Nor would a good innkeeper follow this proportion, but he would rather see how much the person whose upkeep he is charged with brings in. And so, approaching the extreme of excess or deficiency, he will come to the mean of which we are speaking, without stopping at the arithmetic mean, which is relative to the divided thing. Similarly, when physicians prescribe something to eat or drink, they do not look to the proportion and mean of the thing divided in itself, but looking to the person, they will give greater or lesser proportion to his life, without regard for an equal distance between extremes—as though, if eating ten ounces of bread was too much and two ounces too little, they would follow the mean (i.e., six ounces). Rather, their consideration of the person will push them toward the extreme of either excess and deficiency. This proportion, as we have said, is called "geometric," and concerns a reasonable proportion relative to the person, rather than a mean equidistant from two extremes. Thus, if we retain the example of the number six as mean, we can say that six is also a mean between four and nine, even though arithmetically it is not at an equal proportion to and distance from the two. For there clearly are more from six to nine than there are from six to four, but geometrically there is indeed an equal proportion: for just as six is made up of the number four and half of four, so too nine is made of six and half of six. And following this proportion, everyone who has knowledge of and is experienced in any art always avoids excess and deficiency in order to select and retain the mean—albeit not the mean relative to the thing and equidistant to the two extremes, but the mean relative to people, which can be found with reason as measure.

4. The geometric method applies to all arts and sciences, and how moral virtue relates to it and intellectual virtue does not.

The arts and sciences always concern themselves with this geometric mean and always direct their work according to it, thus reaching their perfection so that they might brag and say that nothing can be added to or anything taken away from it, as if to suggest that there is no excess or deficiency there. In doing so they praise the intermediate point and chide the extremes as being vicious. If, therefore, all the arts and sciences concern themselves with the geometric mean, it follows that virtue, which surpasses them in perfection, tends to and consists only in this mean. (I am speaking here of the moral virtues alone, and not the intellectual virtues, since the latter by necessity admit no excess, contrasting in this respect with the affections and acts, where we can indeed speak of excess, deficiency, and a mean. This can be seen in fear, assurance, desire, anger, pity, and, briefly stated, between every pleasure and pain, when it is found more or less than is reasonable.) For the two extremes are vicious, and the mean is virtuous. That is, by the use of one thing or another when needed, by and for those who are fitting, for the right reason, and as appropriate. The same holds true for all acts where excess is vicious, deficiency blameworthy, and the mean esteemed.

5. Virtue is an intermediate point between excess and deficiency, and why it is more difficult to do good than evil.

What we are saying, therefore, is that virtue is an intermediate point between excess and deficiency, aiming always at the mean, apart from which there is only a great diversity of fault and error. For according to the Pythagoreans, vice and evil is an infinite thing, which can occur in an infinite number of ways, while the good is a finite and limited thing, which occurs only in a single and fixed manner and way. Accordingly, it should not surprise us to know that it is considered more difficult to do good than evil. For in just the same way it is more difficult to shoot at the white bull's-eye of the target than beside it, for the very reason that there is only one specific, fixed spot for a good shot, but an infinite number of others for a bad shot. The same applies to doing good and evil, in whatever circumstances it may be, since:

> For doing good there is just a single way,
> but wide open is the field for being led astray.[1]

And indeed, just as no white is applied where you should not shoot, so too the nature of evil is such that it is not presented as something to aim at, but to be missed. The good is thus the white bull's-eye of the target and the bad whatever lies outside that. Consequently, just as the area outside the white bull's-eye has no designated place to aim at, so too there is no rule or precept for doing evil.

---

[1] This unidentified verse is omitted from the 1587 Latin translation. Cf. Matt. 7:13–14.

6. The definition of virtue according to Aristotle, and how not every action or affection in itself admits an intermediate point.

From all that has been said above, we can now easily derive the proper definition of moral virtue, namely, that virtue is a habit acquired by certain judgment and choice, which consists in the mean that is relative to us and is such that the wise would follow it.[2] We have already explained why virtue is a habit by judgment and choice founded on right reason, and why it is a mean between the two vices of excess and deficiency. I am speaking here of virtue considered according to its substance and true definition; for were it to be considered together with vice, it would prove to be an extreme of the good, and vice an extreme of evil. Nevertheless, we should be aware that not every action and affection admits an intermediate point, since some can only be evil and vice. In fact, you only have to name them to recognize them as such: malice, impudence, and envy, and, among actions, adultery, theft, murder, and so on. For all these there is no circumstance of time, place, person, or anything else that can take anything away from them so as to make them a little less vicious, and to identify some intermediate point in them. For if you want to have an intermediate point there, you would have to do the same for timidity, intemperance, and injustice, saying that they admit of an excess, a deficiency, and a mean. It would be the same thing, in fact, as identifying an intermediate point in extremes of excess or deficiency, of too much and too little. But if, just as temperance and strength cannot admit an excess of too much or a deficiency of too little, since the intermediate point is situated somewhere in the extreme and is the summit of mediocrity, so too for the aforementioned things there will be no excess, mean, or deficiency. For in whatever way you do these things, they will always be vice and sin. What we are saying, in short, is that there is no intermediate point in excess or in deficiency, just as there can be no excess or deficiency at the intermediate point.

---

[2] Aristotle, *Nicomachean Ethics* 2.1 (1103a26ff).

7. The definition of virtue condensed, and then appropriated in accordance with Christian doctrine.

This, then, was the definition of virtue as Aristotle gave it to us, and we can distill it further by saying that virtue is a habit that inclines one to act according to right reason. For to say that it is a habit acquired by a certain judgment and choice is already subsumed under the word "habit" since, as we noted above, a habit must come from deliberately performed acts, preceded by a good deliberation and intention, and not haphazardly, by ignorance and without consideration. Furthermore, all that follows thereafter is subsumed under the phrase "that inclines one to act according to right reason," as we demonstrated when we spoke of the geometrical mean, which consists in a proportion made by the compass of reason rather than a certain rule of the mean equidistant from the two extremes of the divided thing. And we understand this natural reason to agree with God's immutable and eternal law imprinted in us, and that the more remote cause of this reason and natural judgment—as well as the remote cause of the will, works, and of the virtue that follows—are recognized to be of God rather than from elsewhere. And even though the depravity and corruption of our nature produces a great foolishness and inability in us, we still retain this natural reason and knowledge, as well as some freedom of will, since God willed that his wisdom and virtues be recognized in us, as we will explain at greater length below. Therefore, if we want to adapt our definition more closely to Christian doctrine, we could say that virtue is a habit produced in us by the Holy Spirit, inclining the will to obedience to God, and standing firm and constant by right reason, in full conformity with his law. And we should note that this virtue tends to no other end than to testify to God of the gratitude and recognition we owe him, and of his will toward humankind, so that he might be glorified by us; also, that we are taught to render our works bright and shining before others, so that they might glorify the Father who is in heaven. This brings us to the end of the definition of moral and Christian virtue.

BOOK THREE

8. The difference between the treatment of things that reside in simple knowledge, and those that reside in action.

It does not suffice, however, just to show in general what virtue is, without proceeding to apply what we have said universally to each virtue particularly and distinctly. For to treat of things that consist in simple knowledge is very different from the way we treat things that consist in action and doing. For the former, we proceed by a general and universal treatment from which we draw necessary conclusions. The latter, however, require an investigation of individual things in their minutest details, so as from them to reach a more certain knowledge of the general. In fact, a universal treatment is in this regard all but useless and fruitless, unless it descends afterwards to the particular, checking in their minutest details what had been proposed indistinctly in the general. For this reason, we will now briefly treat all the virtues, one after the other, and show how each of them consists in an intermediate point.

9. Each virtue taken on its own consists in an intermediate point, and their names and extremes.

Following Aristotle,[3] we will begin with the virtue called "courage," and concur with him that it is easy to see how courage is an intermediate point between fear and audacity. As for those who lack fear and in this sense abandon the mean, they have no name. This is true for several other categories of people as well. Those who surpass the mean by their overconfidence are called audacious, rash, and presumptuous, while those who by too much fear exceed the mean or fall short of it by too little confidence are called fainthearted and cowardly. As regards pleasures and pains, the delights and troubles (not all, but only those that belong to the body and consist primarily in touch, and less in displeasure and pain than in pleasure), the intermediate point is called "temperance" and the excess "intemperance." As for the

---

[3] In sections 9–13 La Place closely follows Aristotle's presentation of the virtues in *Nicomachean Ethics* 2.7–9.

extreme of deficiency, there are very few who sin in this way, such that they too are without a name, although we could call them dull and insensitive. As for "generosity," it pertains to giving and taking, and is an intermediate point between lavishness and avarice. The former belongs to excess and the latter to deficiency, and together they are the two extremes in which people fall short and sin, abandoning the intermediate point in opposite directions. The lavish person exceeds the mean by giving without measure, and falls short of it by not taking from anyone. The avaricious person, on the contrary, is excessive by taking too much, and deficient in giving. There is another virtue that comes close to deficiency, and it is called "magnificence." It differs in that generosity pertains to smaller things, and magnificence to the greater. The excess in this magnificence can be called frivolous expenditure, and the deficiency, stingy charity, which two extremes differ from the extremes of generosity.

There is, moreover, a virtue pertaining to honor and infamy, which is another intermediate point and is called "magnanimity," while its excess is called vainglory or arrogance, and its deficiency, pusillanimity. And just as we said above with respect to magnificence that it differs from generosity in that the one concerns great matters and the other lesser things, so it is with this virtue compared to the virtue that pertains to lesser honors. Now honor can be affected by reason, and the pursuit of it can involve more or less than is stipulated by reason: someone who desires it beyond measure is called ambitious, and the one who cares nothing for it shameless, while those who seek it by reason have no name except that they are modest. For anger, too, there can be excess, deficiency, and a mean, all of which are virtually without name. But because we call a person who holds to a mean in anger gentle, kind, and mild, we could call the intermediate point gentleness, kindness, and mildness. Those who are unreasonably excessive we could call irate, harsh, and moody, and their vice anger, harshness, and moodiness. As for those who lack anger altogether, the French language has no term for them.

There are three other intermediates, which all have in common that they take their place in the very midst of human life and action, but differ among themselves in that the one consists in true things, and the others in what is joyous and pleasant. The intermediate point that consists in true things is the truth, and it is found between boasting and deprecation, the former of which exaggerates and advances, while the latter diminishes and abases. As regards what is joyous and pleasant, those who follow the mean in this are said to be merry and civil, and the intermediate point is merriness and civility. Those, on the other hand, who surpass what is reasonable in this are commonly called jesters and their vice jest, while on the contrary those who are displeased by every conversation, meeting, and pleasantry are called boorish, uncivil, and savage, and the accompanying vice boorishness and incivility. As for everything else pertaining to pleasure in human life, those who please and are fittingly agreeable are called friend, and its mean friendship. Yet those who try to please too much, albeit without seeking to profit from this in any way, are called obsequious, while those who do seek to profit from it are called flatterers. Those who give no thought at all to being pleasant or agreeable to anyone are called difficult and troublesome.

10. The intermediate point that consists in affections and passions, which is nevertheless no virtue.

Nor ought we to forget that there are also intermediate points and means for the affections and passions, and for all that happens in them. Although shame and disgrace are not a virtue, a person who experiences shame and keeps to the mean in this regard is still liable to be praised. For anyone who surpasses that mean is frantic, and he who is deficient on this account is called brazen. "Indignation" is an intermediate point between envy and malice, which are passions revolving around the pleasures and pains that come to us for the good and advancement of another person. Those are properly indignant who are displeased by the advancement of those who are not worthy of it, while the envious are spiteful of the good that comes to another, and the malicious take delight in the evil that overcomes others. As for justice, if it is considered universally and in general, all other virtues will be found to be subsumed under it, and all vices under injustice. But considered particularly as the virtue that renders each person his due, it will be found to be an intermediate point as well. This intermediate point is located in external actions, and at one time follows the geometric proportion and at another time the arithmetic proportion, in different ways. Yet this topic requires a more ample treatment, which we will defer to another time, being content for now with this brief overview whose goal was simply to sketch and draw out the first traits of the virtues, without seeking to fill them out and color them in.

11. The contrariety between the two extremes of the intermediate point and the mean, and the contrariety between the mean and its extremes, and also the resemblance between these extremes and the mean.

Since, therefore, there are in the human affections two extremes, one of which surpasses the mean while the other remains behind it and cannot reach it, with virtue alone being situated in the mean and middle, it appears that they are all each other's opposites—not only the extremes among themselves, but also the extremes over against their mean and the mean over against its extremes.[4] For just as something equal is greater compared to the lesser, but lesser compared to the greater, so too the habits, which are always situated in the middle of both actions and affections, are surpassing and excessive compared to the lesser, but less compared to the greater. We can see this, for example, in the virtue of strength which, relative to timidity and cowardice, seems very much like audacity and rashness, while in comparison to rashness it seems more like timidity than strength. Likewise, a temperate person seems intemperate when compared to a dull person, while they seem dull in comparison to the intemperate. And similarly, the generous approach the avaricious in comparison to the spendthrift, but seem like spendthrifts when they are compared to the avaricious. Accordingly, the extremes each refer to the mean: if the fearful and cowardly call the strong "audacious," the audacious call the strong "timid," and so on.

---

[4] Aristotle, *Nicomachean Ethics* 2.8.

Yet the discrepancy and conflict is much greater and much more apparent between extremes contrasted with each other than it is between the extremes and their mean, inasmuch as there is a greater distance between the extremes than there is between them and the middle. One thus clearly sees that the mean comes closer to the greater and lesser than the lesser to the greater, or the greater to the lesser. And at times there is even some resemblance between the extremes and the mean, as there is between audacity and strength, or lavishness and generosity. But between the extremes themselves there always remains a great difference, since what is at greater distance and separation is ordinarily also more different and contrary. It sometimes also happens that the lesser contrasts more with the mean than the greater does; this is the case with cowardice, which is the lesser and contrasts more with strength than audacity does, which is the greater. The opposite holds true with respect to temperance, as dullness, which is the lesser, differs less from temperance than does intemperance, which is the greater. There are two reasons why this is so, the one relating to the thing, and the other to us: that is, since there is less distance from one of the extremes to the mean than there is from the other extreme to the mean, it is reasonable for there also to be less of a difference, just as we have said of courage, generosity, and lavishness, that the more distant thing differs less. The other reason is that the vices to which we are more inclined by nature seem to be remoter from us than the others, as intemperance seems to us to be more distant from temperance than dullness does, since it is more proper and adapted to one person than to another.

The Right Use of Moral Philosophy

12. The intermediate point that we maintain always inclines more to one extreme than to the other, and the most certain rule for better maintaining the mean in all things.

Since, therefore, virtue is what always tends and leads to the mean, which can be found in affections and actions, it follows that being virtuous is a very difficult thing.[5] For it is not easy and simple to find the mean and intermediate point in everything, just as it is difficult to find the middle of a sphere and circle, except for those who are truly knowledgeable. And the intermediate point we human beings maintain is such that it most often is more inclined to one of the two extremes. Consider, for example, the strength and constancy of Fabius in resisting Hannibal,[6] which comes closer to timidity than rashness, while that of Marius in fighting the Cimbri[7] comes closer to rashness than timidity. So too the generosity of Alexander is closer to lavishness than avarice,[8] while that of Crassus toward the Roman people comes closer to avarice than lavishness.[9] And so the list goes on. And indeed, it is up to each and every one to become angry, to give, and to spend, but it is not up to everyone to become angry with or give to this person, at that time, for that reason, and as is fitting. But the things that are excellent in perfection are generally also rare and praiseworthy. The more certain rule to hold for all who want to keep to the mean in all things is to distance themselves as much

---

[5] Aristotle, *Nicomachean Ethics* 2.9.

[6] Quintus Fabius Maximus Verrucosus (ca. 280–203 BC), as Roman dictator, pursued a policy of attrition against the Carthaginian general Hannibal in 217 BC.

[7] Gaius Marius (ca. 157–86 BC) defeated the Cimbri, a German tribe that had migrated through Europe, near Vercellae in northwestern Italy in 101 BC.

[8] Plutarch recounts Alexander the Great's generosity in a few stories with different variations. Two of these appear in Plutarch, *Regum et imperatorum apophthegmata*, Alexander 4–6 (*Moralia* 179f–180a).

[9] Marcus Licinius Crassus (ca. 115–53 BC), a Roman consul and ally of Julius Caesar, acquired extraordinary wealth through proscriptions and extortion. He wielded significant financial and political power in the late republic.

BOOK THREE

as they can from the most contrary vice they know. This was the very way in which Circe warned Odysseus to steer in the Strait of Messina between the two whirlpools of Charybdis and Scylla, saying:

> Keep your vessel,
> O Odysseus,
> Far from the billowing cloud
> And from that frothing swirl.[10]

For of the two extremes, the one is less vicious than the other. Therefore, since it is so difficult to reach and arrive at this mean, if we cannot obtain it, let us at least push ourselves to follow the lesser evil and what is less vicious, as we have described above.

13. Arming oneself against the vices to which we are most inclined, and especially against delights and pleasures.

Above all, we must diligently guard ourselves against the vices to which we are more susceptible. For by nature we are more inclined to some vices than to others, each of us according to his natural inclination. These vices are easily known by the pleasure or displeasure that comes to us. When we watch carefully, the best remedy will be to withdraw all the way to the side opposite to and in contrast with our vice. For when we are far removed from it, it will be much easier and take less effort to arrive at the mean, as we see with those who want to straighten a crooked and twisted tree. But above all one must be diligent to watch for the delights and pleasures that surprise us even before we can notice them. We must be affected toward pleasure in the same way as the old princes of Troy were toward Helen, while persuading Priam to send her away with the following words:

---

[10] See Homer, *Odyssey* 12.73–110.

The Right Use of Moral Philosophy

> Unrivaled in beauty,
> Sire, Helen may be,
> Esteemed more highly
> Than anything of this world
> —But let us send her back
> To the Greeks.[11]

For once we have dismissed pleasure from us in this way, it will be easier to keep ourselves from falling and to follow the mean—which is indeed something very difficult to prescribe and determine in greater detail, given the variety of circumstances that can present themselves. For example, when it comes to the mean we must hold in anger, we have to consider the people with whom we want to be angry, the cause, the kind of anger, and the time. For at one time we praise those who are gentle in their anger and call them gentle, but afterwards we go on to blame them, and rather praise those who are sharper in their anger, saying that they are more manly and virtuous, and so the list goes on. But as for those who deviate just a little from the mean, whether in excess or deficiency, we should find no fault with them, provided that they go no further than they should. For the greater the distance they keep from the mean and the further back they recede, the more easily they are recognized and known.

14. The view of the Peripatetics and Stoics on the affections and their intermediate points, and how their reasons differ more in word than substance.

It is thus clear that virtue is a habit reducing natural affections and internal motions to an intermediate point between excess and deficiency, and that the Peripatetics' view is therefore better than that of the Stoics, since the latter took away from people all the affections by which they are moved—that is, concupiscence, fear, joy, and sadness—and called them illnesses which, according to their false view, are not so much naturally implanted in man as received. The

---

[11] Homer, *Iliad* 7.350–52.

Peripatetics, on the contrary, maintain that the affections cannot be removed from humankind insomuch as they are innate, and that God and nature (for this is how they say it) by a great providence armed us with these affections, which, since they are often vicious if found in excess, nevertheless can be reduced to a tempered intermediate point. But the Stoics, and after them Cicero[12] and other great men since, among them Lactantius Firmianus[13] and Lorenzo Valla,[14] mocked these intermediate points, saying that they tend to an absurd end where vices are reduced to moderation and where mediocre vices become a virtue, and, moreover, since they do acknowledge the affections of which we just spoke to be vicious, that it is not the affections themselves that ought to be mediocre, but only their causes. In just the same way, they continue, to say that we should not covet or be angry except in a mediocre way is no different from someone saying that we ought not to run too impetuously, but rather go in a mediocre way—and yet, as they point out, someone who proceeds calmly can err, whereas someone else who runs can stay on the straight path. They say that virtue therefore consists in the moderation of causes rather than affections, since affections are moved externally, and that, since affections can just as easily be deficient as excessive, one ought not to moderate them, but rather to assign them specific times, places, and circumstances, lest the things we can use rightly become vice. For so Lactantius says, just as walking on the right path is good and leaving

---

[12] Cicero rejects the Peripatetics' understanding of anger as natural and useful, but he affirms other aspects of their doctrine of the mean. *On Duties*, 1.89.

[13] Lactantius, *Divine Institutes* 6.16.1–6; Lactantius (Lucius Caecilius Firmianus) (ca. AD 250–ca. 330), tutor to Constantine's son Crispus, converted to Christianity around AD 300 and became a Christian apologist.

[14] Lorenzo Valla, *De voluptate ac de vero bono* 3.2, in *Laurentii Vallae Opera* (Basel: Heinrich Petri, 1540), 966–71. Valla (ca. 1406–1457) was an Italian humanist and churchman whose *De voluptate* is a dialogue between a Stoic, an Epicurean, and a Christian. See *The Oxford Dictionary of the Christian Church*, ed. F. L. Cross and E. A. Livingstone, 3rd rev. ed. (Oxford: Oxford University Press, 2005), s.v. "Valla, Lorenzo."

and straying from it is bad, so too being moved by affections toward the good is good, but being moved toward evil is bad.[15] As such, to become angry, to covet, and even to be moved by carnal desire (provided that it is restricted to the marital bed) is not bad, but it is indeed bad to be irate, covetous, and pleasure-seeking. Consequently, he says, we ought not to seek recourse in the moderation and mediocracy of what is implanted in man to keep to the duties that concern human life; rather, we need only come to the guidance and direction of the right way, where the path shall be without any danger, impairment, or obstacle.[16] Here they compare the inward motions to a harnessed coach for which the coachman's main task, in order to drive it straight, consists in knowing the road well, because that is how he will not come upon anything that may hinder or harm him, regardless of how fast he goes. On the contrary, if he is to stick to the road, he ought not, regardless of how gently and lightly he goes, turn aside from the gravel road, or fall into precipices, or go where he need not go.

But if we examine the two views carefully, they prove to differ more in words than substance, since there is in this respect no difference between the right path and the intermediate point, and between the wrong path and the extremes. It is true that in affections that are of themselves vicious, one ought not to look for an intermediate point. For that indeed would be to seek to make a vice an intermediate vice, just as when it comes to the affections that are of themselves good, we need not look for another intermediate point, since we already find ourselves at its highest point, as we have said above. But when it comes to the affections that at different times can be either good or bad (and it is of these that we are properly speaking here), no one can deny—without being contentious—that the intermediate point is that which ought to be held to and ought to be considered virtue, and that "intermediate point" and the "right path" are only different ways of speaking. When this distinction and difference between virtues and vices was made, it was always greatly praised, and followed

---

[15] Lactantius, *Divine Institutes* 6.16.
[16] Lactantius, *Divine Institutes* 6.17.

and greatly lauded by all. This is witnessed by the ancient proverb "Nothing in excess,"[17] as well as the following verses:

> To retain virtue at every point,
> One must always stick to the mean.[18]

And then:

> There is in every situation a certain mean
> For conducting and completing it as one ought:
> Beyond that properly limited point,
> One clearly sees fault and error.[19]

15. Whether according to philosophy it is in us to do good or evil, and whether it is in us to refrain from evil.

From all the reasons we have noted above, the philosophers conclude that people have it in them to do good or evil, and that the virtues and vices are in our power, since we have in us freedom of choice, will, and action, and, consequently, that it depends on us to be good or evil. Now it is true that some suggested that, although it is in our power to do good, it nevertheless is not in us to keep from evil, and that, if no one were good or happy against their wish, it nevertheless does not follow that we are evil against our will. However, the one cannot be confessed without granting the other. For if we grant that it is in us to do good, we must also confess that it is in us not to do it. And if we grant that it is in us not to do good, we must also necessarily

---

[17] Terence, *Andria* 1.1.61 (Latin: *ne quid nimis*).

[18] The Latin translation cites Theognis of Megara, *Elegiac Poems* 2.335–36, which is paraphrased in the French text. Pierre de la Place, *De recto usu moralis philosophiae cum doctrina Christiana collatae, libri tres*, in *Petri Plateani viri clarissimi, in curia parisiensi regiorum subsidiorum, seu vectigalium praesidis primatii, Opuscula* […] ([Geneva]: Eustathius Vignon, 1587), 83.

[19] The Latin translation cites Horace's well-known adage "Est modus in rebus, sunt certi denique fines / Quos ultra citraque nequit consistere rectum" (*Satires* 1.1.106). La Place, *De recto*, in *Opuscula*, 83. The French edition contains a versified paraphrase (from an unidentified source), which is translated here.

grant that it is in us to do evil and, just as we are good voluntarily, we are also evil and wicked voluntarily. Otherwise we have to turn everything we have said around, and say that people do not have the principles and beginnings of either one in them, and that they are not the ones who produce and engender both good and evil acts as fathers beget their children. Now if things are as the philosophers think they are, namely, that the principles and sources of our actions cannot be found anywhere but in us, it indeed follows that the action and exercise of those things whose beginning and foundation is in us resides in us as well. In this respect the philosophers add that there is no one, regardless of how limited his mental capacity is, who cannot know of himself that this is true. Furthermore, they point out that this is witnessed to us by the ordinances and laws made to govern the people, which punish those who do evil and honor those who do good—for no other reason than to incite and stir them up to do good, and to turn them away from evil. For if neither were in our power, of what use would it be to exhort or forbid?

Indeed, everyone understands that it is pure folly and vanity to exhort people to do something that is not in their power, or to forbid what they cannot refrain from doing. For that would be no different than forbidding someone from feeling hot or cold, being hungry or thirsty, or experiencing pleasure or pain. From this they conclude that it is just as much in our power to keep from doing evil as it is to do good. For laws and magistrates were introduced for both, as we have said—and not only to punish people when they do evil knowledgeably, but also when they do so ignorantly, if indeed they are the cause of their own ignorance. Pittacus thus prescribed double punishment for those who do evil when drunk, for the simple reason that the principle and beginning of inebriation, and the resulting action, is found in the person who did it, since it is within human power not to become drunk.[20] By the same account, laws punish those who ignorantly contravene them, inasmuch as everyone ought to know them,

---

[20] Pittacus of Mytilene (ca. 650–570 BC) was a statesman, lawgiver, and sage. For the attribution of the law of double penalty to Pittacus, see Aristotle, *Politics* 2 (1274b19–21). The double penalty also appears in *Nicomachean Ethics* 3.5 (1113b30–33).

BOOK THREE

and ignorance of laws in turn proceeds from us, as is true for all other cases where we are ignorant of things everyone ought to know.

And should someone say that not all people are equally wellborn, since some are more inclined, ready, and likely to stumble according to the diversity of inclinations and natures, which are entirely beyond us and outside of our power, we will be constrained to return to this point—namely, if people are unjust, intemperate, or otherwise wicked, they themselves and nothing else are the sole cause of having developed by their own accord the habit of living unjustly, intemperately, or some other evil way. For the effect (i.e., the habit) corresponds to the efficient cause (i.e., what performs and produces the work). Everyone can see and know this in himself by experience, regardless of the particular activity he considers, inasmuch as he will notice in the end that the habit comes from that activity. For that reason, it would be unreasonable to ignore the fact that habits are made and produced by operations and actions done in each thing, just as it would be unreasonable to say that, while you want to wrong or harm someone, or to perform a pleasurable vice, you do not want to become unjust and intemperate. For to do knowledgeably that from which injustice and intemperance proceeds is no different from voluntarily becoming unjust and intemperate, since someone who wills the cause necessarily wills also the effect that follows.

It is indeed true that once we have become unjust, intemperate, or otherwise vicious by our own fault, it is no longer in us not to be unjust, intemperate, or otherwise vicious, as it was in the beginning. In just the same way, it is not up to the sick to be healthy when it pleases them, having fallen ill by their own fault after they lived in dissolution and intemperance by their own will and accord, and refused to believe the physician. For at the beginning they had greater power not to fall ill, but now that they have abandoned their health and become indifferent to it, it is no longer in their power to escape the illness at will, just as someone who has thrown something into the water can no longer take it back out when he wills, although he indeed could have withheld it before throwing it in. The same applies to those who become intemperate by their own fault, since it was in their power not to adopt this habit and become intemperate. For this reason we have to say that if they are intemperate, they became intemperate voluntarily, and that, once they have become voluntarily intemperate, it is afterwards also not within the power of their will to be intemperate, as it once was. Since, therefore, we reproach those who fall ill by dissolute living but excuse cases of illness that arise naturally or in some other way, we show sufficiently that the vices for which people are reproached are voluntary. For how else can you say that man is subject to reproach because of these vices?

Some still persist in the contrary opinion and say that no one would himself want to be the cause of being wicked and therefore voluntarily will evil, but that the occasion for doing evil comes rather from not everyone having the ability to discern well the end of the work they do, that is, whether it is in itself and truly good or evil. For, so they say, people are deceived by appearances, and therefore, if there are some who do evil and are vicious, this is more by error than free will. They furthermore even insist that it ordinarily happens that things appear to people as they are of their natural inclination, so that, if all are not equally endowed by nature to see and judge the end of the things that present themselves, it follows that vice is to be imputed more to nature than to us. But if it were indeed the case that we are deceived by an appearance, which resembles each of us as we are, and that those who are vicious therefore follow evil more easily, having been deceived by the appearance of goodness—what else can we blame except their habit, which was formed in them by habitual performance of evil according to their free will, choice, and judgment? For we do not deny that inclinations are natural, but we maintain that the operations, as well as the habits engendered by the works they produce, are voluntary.

And should they suggest that they were not habitually vicious, I would like to ask them why they consider vice to be more constrained and forced in them, and by what logic people differ from one another, since choice, judgment, and will are equally free with respect to the good and the wicked. For if nature has given us regard for and knowledge of the end of things, it gave it to us with respect to evil as much as to good, such that one must conclude that nature is the cause either of both or of neither. If nature is the cause of neither, it follows that vice as well as virtue, doing good as well as doing evil, are voluntary.

BOOK THREE

And, if nature is the cause of both, it also follows that we perform both virtue and vice naturally rather than voluntarily—but we cannot say this. Yet however one understands this, one cannot deny that the good or evil operations in us are voluntary. Both the one and the other proceed from choice, which is free and in its liberty, such that when we do something, we do it because we will it thus. When we refrain from doing it, this is also because we do not will it. Accordingly, the habit engendered from our works is the cause of our being virtuous or vicious, and our being virtuous or vicious is the cause of the true or false appearance of the end. Consequently, both doing good and doing evil depend on us. For we are as are our habits are, and, as we are, so is the end we assign to our works. But if they could, people prefer to call themselves the cause of good, while making the cause of evil external to themselves and imputing all the blame to nature, that is, to God himself, who has made nature as it is. In this respect Homer said through the person of Jupiter:

> My word, how mortals take the gods to task!
> All their afflictions come from us, we hear.
> And what of their own failings? Greed and folly
> double the suffering in the lot of man.[21]

Plato agreed with this, and in establishing his republic says that above all else we must make sure that no one, whether old or young, says or thinks in any way or form that God is the cause of evil, that is, of sin, since such an expression is unfortunate and detestable, repugnant to all truth, and most pernicious to all those who receive it.[22]

---

[21] Homer, *Odyssey* 1.32–35. The French text cites from Jacques Peletier du Mans's translation of the first two books of the *Odyssey*. See *Oeuvres poétiques de Jacques Peletier* (Paris: Michel de Vascosan, 1547), 12. This English translation is from Robert Fitzgerald, trans., *The Odyssey* (London: Heinemann, 1961).

[22] Plato, *Republic* 2.379a–380c.

The Right Use of Moral Philosophy

16. Comparison between Christian doctrine and philosophy on the will to do good and the will to do evil, and how philosophy has failed to recognize the source and cause of human sin.

Now, regardless of the extent to which moral philosophy seems to agree with Christian doctrine in locating the cause of sin in man, there nevertheless is this great difference between them: philosophy has never known the source of the evil and folly that is in the human race. But Christian doctrine teaches that God created the first man good and righteous, and that, failing to persevere in the integrity of his nature, he disobeyed God of his own accord, having been created in a condition of liberty and freedom (regardless of how great a role the devil's suggestion played). It also teaches that the first sin was the root, source, and birth of sin in the world, planted in our nature and flowing down even to us. It is by this sin that reason and mind have been obscured and so enveloped by darkness that carnal man, as Paul says, does not understand the things of the Spirit of God,[23] and that the will has been so corrupted, debilitated, and weakened that it is fully enslaved to sin, ready and inclined to all evil. For this reason, we must not seek the cause of vice and sin anywhere but in ourselves, since all actual sin is voluntary and, according to Saint Augustine, even original sin is voluntary by reason of the enjoyment we take in it.[24] God, on the other contrary, is the enemy and adversary of every kind of wickedness we see.

There is also a great difference between Christian doctrine and moral philosophy with regard to what pertains to the cause of virtue and the good. For the word of God does not teach an appearance and mask of virtue, but it rather teaches us a true virtue which, implanted in us by the Holy Spirit, produces outward fruits by which God is glorified in us. Philosophy, on the other hand, never goes beyond external appearances (as has already been said) and what pertains merely to external, civil, and political acts in which human justice consists, that is, the external discipline by which the non-regenerate externally per-

---

[23] 1 Cor. 2:14.

[24] Cf. Augustine, *Retractions* 1.14.2; Augustine, *True Religion* 14, 27.

form their upright works. Moreover, Holy Scripture teaches us a true and spiritual virtue that by our nature we cannot perform, since we cannot choose, will, or accomplish it of ourselves. But when it comes to the works of moral philosophy (i.e., those relating merely to the present life), we do have some measure of free choice, judgment, and will to do or not to do them, and by it we give preference to the upright and virtuous over the vile and wicked. This was how Alexander the Great could keep his hands and even his eyes from Persian women, saying—notwithstanding the lust that otherwise inflamed his heart—that they hurt the eyes of those who look at them.[25] The same is true of Scipio's ability to control himself and to keep from touching other men's wives,[26] Fabricius when he resisted corruption by the gifts of Pyrrhus,[27] and others.

In all of this we must nevertheless consider that, just as God adorned the pagans with beautiful virtues, he also bridled them with a view to the preservation of the human race, which would not have remained if the boiling impetuosities of our corrupted nature had been allowed to run their course. Accordingly, whenever we speak of human strength in matters that concern the present life and its maintenance, we always understand the need to recognize God's grace in all these things. For without his grace it would be impossible for the little strength that is in us to nourish and sustain tranquility and human society. In this regard, therefore, we ought to steer a middle course between the two extremes represented by those who attribute too much to the human race, and by the others who remove from it all will entirely. The latter seek to reduce us to Stoic necessity, a great danger to the discipline of this life, to which we must diligently hold with both hands. For nothing dampens and cools application to doing good more (while

[25] Plutarch, *Lives. Alexander* 21.5.

[26] Livy, *History of Rome* 26.49–50. Publius Cornelius Scipio Africanus (d. 183 BC) was a famed Roman military commander and politician. Under his leadership the Romans defeated the Carthaginians in Spain and Africa.

[27] Plutarch, *Lives. Pyrrhus* 18.1–5. Gaius Fabricius Luscinus (3rd c. BC) was a Roman consul and censor. He is often presented as an example of ancient frugality and honor.

leading to the abandonment of all discipline and every rule of life) than the positing of such a necessity, which overturns all discipline as something useless and without benefit, while the very opposite is in fact true. If discipline were indeed so useless, why would it be so carefully recommended throughout Scripture? And should there only be the composition of the human body as it is, and the experience that each person himself can have of it, it ought to suffice to make us confess that there is in us freedom of external and outward movement. For no one can say that the virtue of seeing, reading, hearing, and moving, of doing or refraining from certain works and acts is outside of himself. To deny that choice and will retain some freedom in us is therefore tantamount to denying something of which we ourselves sense the contrary. And as for the freedom God willed to leave in us, regardless of how weakened and debilitated it may be, it was (as we have said) to preserve human society, as we accustom ourselves to discipline and exercise ourselves in it, which would indeed be impossible if our will were entirely enslaved and constrained without any freedom. And since God, furthermore, left our nature some sense and knowledge of the difference between what is good and what is wicked and vicious, we can well judge that he also left us some freedom to aspire to what is good and suitable for the maintenance of this life.

17. The great impediment to the freedom of the human will in matters pertaining to the present life, and how one ought to profit from the fall of great men.

I do not, however, want to skip over the fact that this freedom of the human will is severely hindered by the impetuosity of our affections. At times this impetuosity is of the sort that is so strong that it pushes the will to will as if by force. Or, to express it more clearly, this impetuosity pulls and drags the will along, preventing it from obeying the reason it knows so well. And yet, one ought not to excuse it for voluntarily letting itself go. This is why Medea said:

What is good, that I see and desire:
And yet, I leave the good, and take the evil.[28]

The devil's temptations and suggestions are of the sort that are so strong and violent that they set people afire or push them into great fury and wickedness. And yet, the will clearly yields to and agrees with it. For Nero, to mention just one example, regardless of how much he was pushed by the devil, still would not have performed the cruelties and miseries he did if he had not willed them. And what we frequently read and see happening to the greatest, wisest, and most virtuous and prudent—namely, that they, like David, Solomon, and others, sometimes fall deeply—clearly shows how great is the weakness or perversity of our natural will. For if these great men, who were trained in piety and the fear of God, or rather learned to subdue their desires and evil affections so well, were still unable to subject them as they ought to have, how shall the will of the profane and unbelieving not readily run to evil? Yet such mistakes ought to serve as examples to us and warnings against human folly, so that we might unceasingly ask God for the aid promised his church. This he has commanded us to do, so that by his aid we may exercise our faith in him all the more, and know better by experience how he is always nearby and helping us.

18. Internal and spiritual movements are not from us.

It is to this extent that we can accord something to man as far as external and moral discipline are concerned, which therefore is not beyond human power at all—where we understand "discipline" only as the external and visible acts pertaining to human justice, as we have so often said. For when it comes to the internal and spiritual movements and acts, which do not happen without the movement of the Holy Spirit (e.g., true fear of God; true confidence in him, which overcomes all fear and terror, even of death; dilection, constancy, and perseverance in the confession of his holy name; and resistance against the desires and harmful affections of pleasure, ambition, envy, vengeance, and

---

[28] Ovid, *Metamorphoses* 7.20.

the like), certainly such movements and acts most agreeable to God cannot come from us or from anywhere else but from God's Holy Spirit. And so the Holy Spirit by his efficacy turns the bridle, so to speak, of our will—which due to our natural corruption can of itself only run to what is vicious and evil—to what is good and holy. He directs our will on this path, such that the consent to do good that follows cannot be called natural, but must be said to proceed from God's grace. It is, therefore, with good reason that those who come to Christ are drawn by the Father.[29] And regardless of how much we feel the power of God to be at work in us, from our side there is nevertheless always much resistance, and the faith given to us by God is surrounded by great unbelief. He felt this who said, "I believe, Lord, but help my unbelief."[30] We can conclude from this that God does not remove the freedom of our will, but rather gives our will its freedom, since he pulls the will out from under the yoke of sin, and inclines it to seek holiness and righteousness.

19. Whether it is possible for people to act according to God's law, and how statesmen ought to take no offense at this teaching.

Should someone, therefore, ask whether people have it in them to do good (i.e., to keep the law of God according to Christian doctrine), one can only answer this question properly if the extent of sin and natural human infirmity is first carefully considered, and if we also understand how God's law is not content with the external work required by moral philosophy. Rather, we must understand that it demands also a perfect and continual obedience and consent from man's entire inner nature in full conformity with it—which is impossible for us, given that we are filled with doubt, distrust, and contempt for God, and are furthermore pushed by an infinite number of evil and perverse affections. For this reason, those who sought to apply the abovementioned logic of philosophy here (i.e., that it would be vanity and folly to command or forbid what is not in human power, inferring

---

[29] See John 6:44.
[30] Mark 9:24.

from this that the law of God is not impossible to the human race) were quite mistaken. For the logic of moral and political philosophy is to command that its orders really be carried out. But the principal cause and logic of the law of God is that the wrath of God against sin might be clearly demonstrated and made known to all, accusing all people so as to convict them of death and eternal damnation by God's untainted justice.

The second reason does indeed conform with that of political philosophy, namely, that everyone do what it commands, albeit only as we have described above, where we discussed the way good and righteous works can be performed. As long as people are more philosophical and political than Christian in their constitution, they take offense at this. But if they consider the matter more closely, they will find that it all goes back to the exaltation of the benefit of Jesus Christ, since it is not possible to attribute to human strength this power to perform and accomplish God's law by human strength, and to hold on to his grace announced by the gospel. For to those who can justify themselves by their works of the law, Jesus Christ is useless and came for nothing.

20. The order of virtues maintained by Cicero differs from Aristotle's.

This, then, brings us to the end of our brief, Christian discussion of the moral virtues, and of our succinct listing of these virtues in various types and kinds according to the diversity of human affections and actions, as well as the differences between the tasks and duties specific to each individual person. These pertain to the preservation of nature and lend themselves to the government and preservation of human life and society, since it is certain that people by their natural political constitution are created and engendered for it, and many of their actions tend to this end. Accordingly, in line with the order of virtues Cicero maintains in his *On Duties*, which diverges from that of Aristotle, it follows that man must above all else be clothed and adorned with justice, which punishes the wicked and protects the good, regulates their contracts and conventions, and, in sum, renders to each his due.[31] Next, this justice must be bolstered with strength and constancy, so as to resist virtuously all impediments to the contrary. And it must be accompanied by beneficence and generosity, since it is impossible to maintain human society if there is no reciprocal and mutual communication of free offices and tasks among people, followed by the gratitude and recognition naturally owed by those who received aid and favor from others. Friendship is included on the same level, but it is surpassed by the charity or even piety that fathers and mothers show for their children, or of children for their fathers and mothers, or for others who hold the place of fathers and superiors. As for all the other virtues, they pertain to the way all people individually conduct their private and personal life, so that they may moderate their excessive desires and affections.

To conclude, therefore, we hold that we have now fulfilled what we proposed at the outset, and sufficiently demonstrated what the sovereign good of the human race is like, to which people must direct all their acts. It consists in virtue, and we have demonstrated how it can be acquired and offered a definition and exposition. We have shown how this is applied to a variety of different human acts and affections, and so explained the difference between moral philosophy and Christian doctrine, as well as its proper use. Finally, we have demonstrated the harm that arises when the two are confused.

---

[31] Cicero, *On Duties* 1.15.

INDEX

Abel, 56
affections, xxxi–xxxii, 47–48, 52–53, 54
  freedom and, 88–89
  intermediate points, 78–81
  virtue and, 63–64, 65, 73–74
  will and, 88–89
Alexander the Great, 76, 87
Amboise Conspiracy, xvi–xvii
Amboise, Edict of, xxi, xxviii
anger, 72–73, 78, 79
Antoine, king of Navarre, xvii
archery metaphor, 17, 68
architecture, science of, 16, 24
Aristides, 51, 55
Aristophanes, 3
Aristotle, xxix, xxxii, 5, 52
  felicity, xxx, 22–23, 24, 29–31
  moral philosophy, 13–14, 18
  soul, human, 37, 48
  virtue, xxxi, 38–39, 69, 70, 71, 91–92
arithmetic mean, xxxii, 18, 66–67, 74
Arnobius, 14–15
arts, 49–50, 51, 67–68
Augsburg, Confession of, xviii
Augustine of Hippo, xxix, 86

Beza, Theodore, xviii, xxii, xxvii–xxviii
Bible, Scripture, xxiii, 4–6, 86–87, 88
Buisson, Albert, xxvii

Cabanel, Patrick, xxii–xxiii
Calvinists, xxiii
Calvin, John, xv, xvii, xxvi, xxvii–xxviii
Cato the Elder, 55
Charles IX, xvii–xx, xxi, xxvii
choice, 52–53, 54, 69, 88
Christ. *See* Jesus Christ
Christian doctrine, xxxi, 39–40
  felicity, 24–27, 29–31
  good works, xxxi, 26–27, 28, 43
  moral philosophy and, xxx–xxxi,
    7, 13–15, 43, 55–60, 70,
    86–88, 90–91
  Plato, Platonism, 14–15
Christian righteousness, 55–57
Cicero, xx, 4–5, 12, 79, 91–92
Clement of Alexandria, xxviii, 14
Condé, prince of, Louis de Bourbon,
  xvi–xvii, xix, xxi
contemplation, 22–23, 25
courage, 71, 75
Crassus, Marcus Licinius, 76

d'Albret, Jeanne, queen of Navarre,
  xxiv, xxv
Daussy, Hugues, xxi, xxii
David, 89
deficiency, 12, 22, 66–68, 69, 72, 78
deliberation, 52–53, 54

93

Index

de Medici, Catherine, xvi, xvii–xviii, xix, xx–xxi, xxvii
Democritus, 35
d'Este, Ippolito, xviii, xxvii
devil, the, 86, 89
dilection, 58–59
Diogenes the Stoic, 4
discipline, 87–88, 88–90
displeasure, pain, 20–21, 45–46, 48–49
divine law, xxvii, 4–6, 21, 39, 43, 58, 70, 90–91
du Bourg, Anne, xxiii

education, xix–xx, 42, 46
end, final, 16–18, 22, 27
   honor, 21–22, 47
   pleasure, 20–21, 28–29, 47
   virtue, 24–25, 28–30
Epictetus, 51
Epicurus, Epicureans, xxix, 14, 20–21
ethics, xxix, 11–13. *See also* moral philosophy
evil, 27, 29, 86
   choice, 52–53
   doing, xxxii, 46, 49, 55, 64, 82–85
   good and, 12, 26
   habits and, 83–85
   moral, 86–88
   pleasure and, 21, 28–29, 49
   refraining from, 81–84
   vice and, 48, 68, 69
excess, 12, 44, 66–69, 71–72, 78–79, 81
extremes, xxxii, 44, 65–68, 70, 71–72, 74–75, 80

Fabius Maximus Verrucosus, Quintus, 55, 76
Fabricius Luscious, Gaius, 87
faith, 40, 56–57, 60
felicity, xxix, 19–20, 21–22, 27
   Christian doctrine, 24–27, 29–31
   contemplation, 22–23, 25

pleasure, 20–21
   in soul, 28–29
   sovereign good, 19–20, 22, 28–29, 30–31
forced acts, 54–55
Foxe's *Book of Martyrs*, xxv–xxvi
France, 6n5
   parlement of Paris, xv, xvii, xviii, xxiii, xxvii
Francis I, xv
Francis II, xvi, xvii, xxi, xxvii
freedom, 54, 81, 86, 88–89
free will, 58, 70, 84, 90
friends, friendship, 73, 92

generosity, 72, 74–75, 76
geometric mean, xxxii, 66–67, 67–68, 70, 74
Gilmont, Jean-François, xxii
God, xxx, 12, 57–58, 70, 85
   goodness, xxx–xxxi, 59
   glory, xxxi, 28–30, 47, 56–57, 70, 86
   grace, 57–58, 59, 87, 90–91
   image, humans created in, 12, 40
   knowledge of, 24–27, 29–31, 39, 58
   law of, xxvii, 4–6, 21, 39, 43, 58, 70, 90–91
   will, 30–31, 70
good, 16, 35, 68, 85
   evil and, 12, 26
   highest, xxix–xxx
   sovereign, 19–20, 22, 28–29, 30–31
good works, xxxii–xxxiii, 49–52, 81–82, 90–91
   Christian, xxxi, 26–27, 28, 43
   justification and, 55–57
   morality and, 43–44
   moral philosophy, 55–56, 57, 59–60, 81–82
   pleasure in, 45, 47, 51
   righteousness and, 57–60
   virtue and, 41–42, 43–45

Index

gospel, the, 39, 47–48
Goulart, Simon de, xxv–xxvi
glory of God, xxxi, 28–30, 47, 56–57, 70, 86
grace, 57–58, 59, 87, 90–91
Greek, ancient philosophy, xxviii, 13–15, 16, 24–25, 55–57. *See also* moral philosophy; individual philosophers
Guise, Francis, duke of, Guises, xvi–xvii, xviii–xix, xxvii

habits, 42–43, 45–46, 48
  evil and, 83–85
  virtue and, 45–46, 50, 58, 63–65, 69, 70
heart, human, xxxi, 36–37, 52, 56, 87
Heraclitus, 48–49
heresies, heretics, xxix, 6, 14–15
  Protestants as, xvi, xxviii
Hesiod, 18
Holy Spirit, xxxi, 31, 48, 70, 86
Homer, *Iliad*, 77–78
  Odyssey, 77, 85
honor, xxx, 47, 72
  final end, 21–22, 47
Horace, 81
Huguenots, French, xvii–xviii, xviii–xix, xxi–xxii, xxvii
  Massacre of Vassy, xviii–xix, xxvii
  See also Protestants

ignorance, 54–55, 58, 82–83
intellectual virtue, 38–40, 67–68
intemperance, 45, 71–72, 75, 83–84
intermediate point, 65, 67–68, 69, 71–75, 76–77, 80. *See also* mean

Jesus Christ, xxx, 56, 91
  gospel, 39, 47–48
  knowledge of God, 25–27, 31, 40
judgment, 50, 54, 55, 59, 69, 70

justice, xxviii, 3–4, 5, 43, 53, 73–74, 91–92
  divine, xxvii, 4–6, 21, 39, 43, 58, 70, 90–91
justification, 55–60
  good works and, 55–57
  reason and, 55–57, 58, 59–60
Justinian, *Institutiones*, xv
Justin Martyr, xxviii, 5, 14

Kim, Seong-Hak, xxvii
knowledge, 23–24, 49–50, 71, 76, 80
  of God, 24–27, 29–31, 39, 40, 58

Lactantius Firmianus, 79–80
La Place, Pierre de,
  Commentaires, xxi–xxiv
  education treatises, xix–xx
  as lawyer, *Cour des aides*, Paris, xv–xvi, xix, xxi, xxv, 3–4
  monarchy, xx–xxi
  Reformed Christianity, xv–xvi, xix, xxii, xxiv–xxv, xxxii–xxxiii
  Right Use of Moral Philosophy, xxvi–xxvii, xxviii–xxxiii
St. Bartholomew's Day Massacre, xv, xxv–xxvi, xxxi
L'Hôpital, Michel de, xvii, xxii, xxvii–xxviii, xxxiii, 3, 7
Lorraine, cardinal of, Charles Guise, xiv, xxvii

Marius, Gaius, 76
Massacre of Vassy, xviii–xix, xxvii
mathematical sciences, 18, 67–68
mean, 65, 66–68, 69, 72–75
  arithmetic, xxxii, 18, 66–67, 74
  geometric, xxxii, 66–67, 67–68, 70, 74
  holding to, 44–45, 47–48, 78, 81
  See also intermediate point
Medea, 88–89

95

Index

medical, health, 16, 36, 44, 46, 51, 66–67, 83
mediocrity, 69, 79–80
military art, 16
moderation, xxxii, 44, 47, 79–80
monarchy, xx–xxi
moral evil, 86–88
moral law, xxxii–xxxiii
moral philosophy, 47
    Christian doctrine and, xxx–xxxi, 7, 13–15, 43, 55–60, 70, 86–88, 90–91
    definition, xxix–xxx
    evil, 86–88
    good works, 55–56, 57, 59–60, 81–82
    justification, 55–57, 59
    natural law, 12–13
    sovereign good, 16–19
    theology and, 57–58, 59
    See also individual Greek philosophers; Greek schools
morals, 11, 13, 53, 90–91
morals, science of, 11–13, 36
    students of, 17–18
moral virtue, 38–39, 41–42, 67–68, 69, 91–92

natural inclination, 16, 21, 36, 41–42, 48
    vices, 77–78, 84
natural law, xxviii, xxix, 4, 12–13
Navarre, Antoine de, xvi, xxii
Nero, 89

Ockham, William of, 58–59
opinion, 53
Origen, xxviii–xxix, 14–15

parlement of Paris, xv, xvii, xviii, xxiii, xxvii
Paul, Saint, 15, 57, 86

Pelagian, semi-, xxxii
Peripatetics, xxxii, 78–80
Philip II of Spain, xvii
philosophy, xxviii
    felicity, xxx–xxxi, xxxi
    Greek, ancient, xxviii, 13–15, 16, 24–25, 55–57
    law and, 3–6, 82
    theology and, 6–7
    See also moral philosophy
Phocion, 55
Pittacus of Mytilene, 82
Plato, xxix, 46
    Christian doctrine and, 14–15
    felicity, good, xxx, 23–24
    human nature, soul, 36–37, 41
    Idea, 23–24, 38
    moral philosophy, 11, 13–14, 85
Platonists, xxviii–xxix
pleasure, 20–21, 37, 42, 48–49, 53, 72–73
    abstaining from, 44–45
    evil and, 21, 28–29, 49
    as final end, 20–21, 28–29, 47
    in good works, 45, 47, 51
    habit and, 45–46
    seeking, xxix–xxx
    vice and, 77–78
Poissy, Colloquy of, xviii, xxii, xxvii
political, civil science, 3–4, 19, 55, 60, 91–92
    civil law, xxviii, 3–4
    felicity, 21–22
    morals, 11, 13, 90–91
    theology and, 5–6
    virtues, 38, 42, 43
Porphyry, 15
power, human, 63–64, 65, 81–83, 89
Protestantism, Protestants, xv–xvi, xvi–xvii, xvii–xix, xxvii
    as heretics, xvi, xxviii
    See also Huguenots, French

Index

punishment, 46, 82–83
Pythagoras, Pythagoreans, 26, 41, 68

reason, human, 16, 20–21, 30–31, 52–53, 54, 88–89
   justification and, 55–57, 58, 59–60
   knowledge of God, 25–26, 39
   virtue and, 37–38, 50, 70, 72
Reformed Christianity, xv–xvi, xix, xxii, xxiv–xxv, xxvii
   election, xxiv–xxv
righteousness, 26, 55–60
Roman Catholics, Catholicism, xx, xxiii
   Colloquy of Poissy, xviii, xxii
   Protestantism and, xv–xvi, xvi–xvii, xvii–xix, xxvii

St. Bartholomew's Day Massacre, xv, xxv–xxvi, xxxi
St. Germain, Edict of, xviii, xxvii
St. Germain, Peace of, xxv
scholastics, 57–60
sciences, 11, 19, 67–68
   mathematics, 18, 67–68
   See also political, civil science
Scipio Africanus, Publius Cornelius, 87
Scotus, John Duns, 58–59
Scripture, xxiii, 4–6, 86–87, 88
self-preservation, 20–21
sin, 21, 26, 39, 40, 54–55, 56, 72
   cause of, 86–88
   extent of, 90–91
   mortal, 57–58, 59
Socrates, 13, 41
Solomon, 89
soul, human, 48, 63–64
   divisions, 36–37, 41
   felicity and, 28–29
sovereign good, 16–19, 41
   felicity, 19–20, 22, 28–29, 30–31

pleasure, 20–21
Stoics, xxix, xxxii, 4, 27, 28
   affection, xxiii, 47, 78–80, 87
   moral philosophy, 14, 41
   virtue, 47–48
strength, human, 69, 74–75, 76, 87, 91

temperance, 44–45, 53, 69, 71–72, 74–75
Terence, 81
Tertullian, xxviii, xxix, 5, 6, 15
Theognis of Megara, 81
theology, 3–7
   moral philosophy and, 57–58, 59
   See also Christian doctrine
Trent, Council of, xxviii
truth, 30, 73

Valla, Lorenzo, 79
Varro, Marcus Terentius, xxix, 19–20
vice, 38, 48, 68, 73, 75, 79–80
   evil and, 48, 68, 69
   natural inclinations, 77–78, 84
   pleasure and, 77–78
   virtue and, 42, 43, 44, 64, 80–81
   voluntary, 82–85, 86
virtue, xxxi–xxxii, 12, 47–48
   acquisition, developing, 41–42, 44–46, 49
   acts of, 22–23
   affections and, 63–64, 65, 73–74
   cause of, 86–87
   definition, 64, 69–71
   final end, 24–25, 28–30
   God, knowledge of, 24–27
   good works and, 41–42, 43–45
   habit of, 45–46, 50, 58, 63–65, 69, 70
   intellectual, 38–40, 67–68
   knowledge of, 23–24
   moral, 38–39, 41–42, 67–68, 69, 91–92

INDEX

nature of, 48–49, 65–68
principal intellectual, 38–40
reason and, 37–38, 50, 70, 72
vice and, 42, 43, 44, 64, 80–81
will to, 50, 52–55, 56–57, 59–60
virtuous, being, 76–77
vocation, xx, 3–4, 23
voluntary acts, 54–55, 81–82, 83–85, 88
vice, 82–85, 86

wicked acts, 26, 42, 46, 54, 82, 84, 86, 89
wicked, the, 37, 54–55, 83–84, 91
will, human, 83–85, 86–88
   affections and, 88–89
   free, 58, 70, 84, 90
   Holy Spirit and, 89–90
   to virtue, 50, 52–55, 56–57, 59–60
wisdom, 28, 70

Sources in Early Modern Economics, Ethics, and Law

Titles Available in the Second Series

On the Law of Nature: A Demonstrative Method
Niels Hemmingsen

On the Duty to Keep Faith with Heretics
Martinus Becanus

The Right Use of Moral Philosophy
Pierre de la Place

Titles Available in the First Series

A Treatise on the Alteration of Money
Juan de Mariana

On the Law in General
Girolamo Zanchi

On Law and Power
Johannes Althusius

On Exchange and Usury
Thomas Cajetan

On Righteousness, Oaths, and Usury: A Commentary on Psalm 15
Wolfgang Musculus

On Exchange: An Adjudicative Commentary
Martín de Azpilcueta

A Treatise on Money
Luis de Molina

The Mosaic Polity
Franciscus Junius

Of the Law of Nature
Matthew Hale

On Sale, Securities, and Insurance
Leonardus Lessius

www.ingramcontent.com/pod-product-compliance
Lightning Source LLC
Chambersburg PA
CBHW030334100526
44592CB00010B/698